SELF-LEARNING MANAGEMENT SERIES

VIBRANT
PUBLISHERS

ARTIFICIAL INTELLIGENCE

YOU ALWAYS WANTED TO KNOW

From core AI concepts to practical use—
A guide for future-ready, data-driven thinkers

I0500253

KARTHIK CHANDRAKANT

ARTIFICIAL INTELLIGENCE
ESSENTIALS YOU ALWAYS WANTED TO KNOW

First Edition

Published by Vibrant Publishers LLC, USA, www.vibrantpublishers.com

Paperback ISBN 13: 978-1-63651-638-7
Ebook ISBN 13: 978-1-63651-639-4
Hardback ISBN 13: 978-1-63651-640-0

Library of Congress Control Number: 2025946514

This publication is designed to provide accurate and authoritative information regarding the subject matter covered. The Author has made every effort in the preparation of this book to ensure the accuracy of the information. However, information in this book is sold without warranty, either expressed or implied. The Author or the Publisher will not be liable for any damages caused or alleged to be caused either directly or indirectly by this book.

All trademarks and registered trademarks mentioned in this publication are the property of their respective owners. These trademarks are used for editorial and educational purposes only, without intent to infringe upon any trademark rights. This publication is independent and has not been authorized, endorsed, or approved by any trademark owner.

Vibrant Publishers' books are available at special quantity discounts for sales promotions, or for use in corporate training programs. For more information, please write to bulkorders@vibrantpublishers.com

Please email feedback/corrections (technical, grammatical, or spelling) to spellerrors@vibrantpublishers.com

Vibrant publishes in a variety of print and electronic formats and by print-on-demand. Some material included with standard print versions of this book may not be included in e-books in print-on-demand. To access the complete catalog of Vibrant Publishers, visit www.vibrantpublishers.com

Exclusive Online Resources for You

As our valued reader, your purchase of this book includes access to exclusive online resources designed to enhance your learning experience. These resources can be downloaded from our website, www.vibrantpublishers.com, and are created to help you apply AI concepts and strategies in practical, measurable ways.

Online resources for this book include the following:

1. **Deep Learning Interview Questions:** A collection of commonly asked questions covering essential deep learning topics, preparing you for interviews by exploring core concepts, techniques, and real-world applications.

2. **Machine Learning Interview Questions:** Curated machine learning questions with detailed answers, providing not only effective responses but also insight into the reasoning behind each answer.

3. **Scenario-Based Deep Learning and Machine Learning Questions:** These questions assess your ability to apply deep learning and machine learning concepts to practical problems, encouraging critical thinking on algorithmic and model usage.

4. **Scenario-Based AI Leadership and Strategy Questions:** Designed for leadership roles, this resource focuses on the strategic use of AI, helping you leverage AI for decision-making, innovation, and business alignment.

Why these online resources are valuable:

- **Interview Preparation:** Prepares you for interviews with a thorough understanding of deep learning, machine learning, and AI leadership concepts.

- **In-Depth Knowledge:** Provides clear answers and explanations to ensure mastery of complex AI topics.
- **Critical Thinking Application:** Strengthens your problem-solving skills by encouraging critical thinking through scenario-based questions, allowing you to apply your knowledge effectively.

How to access your online resources:

1. **Visit the website:** Go to www.vibrantpublishers.com
2. **Find your book:** Navigate to the book's product page via the "Shop" menu or by searching for the book title in the search bar.
3. **Request the resources:** Scroll down to the "Request Sample Book/Online Resource" section.
4. **Enter your details:** Enter your preferred email ID and select "Online Resource" as the resource type. Lastly, select "user type" and submit the request.
5. **Check your inbox:** The resources will be delivered directly to your email.

Alternatively, for quick access: simply scan the QR code below to go directly to the product page and request the online resources by filling in the required details.

Happy learning!

SELF-LEARNING MANAGEMENT SERIES

TITLE	PAPERBACK* ISBN

BUSINESS AND ENTREPRENEURSHIP

TITLE	PAPERBACK* ISBN
BUSINESS COMMUNICATION ESSENTIALS	9781636511634
BUSINESS ETHICS ESSENTIALS	9781636513324
BUSINESS LAW ESSENTIALS	9781636511702
BUSINESS PLAN ESSENTIALS	9781636511214
BUSINESS STRATEGY ESSENTIALS	9781949395778
ENTREPRENEURSHIP ESSENTIALS	9781636511603
INTERNATIONAL BUSINESS ESSENTIALS	9781636513294
PRINCIPLES OF MANAGEMENT ESSENTIALS	9781636511542

COMPUTER SCIENCE AND TECHNOLOGY

TITLE	PAPERBACK* ISBN
BLOCKCHAIN ESSENTIALS	9781636513003
CYBERSECURITY ESSENTIALS	9781636514888
MACHINE LEARNING ESSENTIALS	9781636513775
PYTHON ESSENTIALS	9781636512938

DATA SCIENCE FOR BUSINESS

TITLE	PAPERBACK* ISBN
BUSINESS ANALYTICS ESSENTIALS	9781636514154
BUSINESS INTELLIGENCE ESSENTIALS	9781636513362
DATA ANALYTICS ESSENTIALS	9781636511184

FINANCIAL LITERACY AND ECONOMICS

TITLE	PAPERBACK* ISBN
COST ACCOUNTING & MANAGEMENT ESSENTIALS	9781636511030
FINANCIAL ACCOUNTING ESSENTIALS	9781636510972
FINANCIAL MANAGEMENT ESSENTIALS	9781636511009
MACROECONOMICS ESSENTIALS	9781636511818
MICROECONOMICS ESSENTIALS	9781636511153
PERSONAL FINANCE ESSENTIALS	9781636511849
PRINCIPLES OF ECONOMICS ESSENTIALS	9781636512334

*Also available in Hardback & Ebook formats

SELF-LEARNING MANAGEMENT SERIES

TITLE	PAPERBACK* ISBN

HR, DIVERSITY, AND ORGANIZATIONAL SUCCESS

DIVERSITY, EQUITY, AND INCLUSION ESSENTIALS	9781636512976
DIVERSITY IN THE WORKPLACE ESSENTIALS	9781636511122
HR ANALYTICS ESSENTIALS	9781636510347
HUMAN RESOURCE MANAGEMENT ESSENTIALS	9781949395839
ORGANIZATIONAL BEHAVIOR ESSENTIALS	9781636512303
ORGANIZATIONAL DEVELOPMENT ESSENTIALS	9781636511481

LEADERSHIP AND PERSONAL DEVELOPMENT

DECISION MAKING ESSENTIALS	9781636510026
INCLUSIVE LEADERSHIP ESSENTIALS	9781636514765
INDIA'S ROAD TO TRANSFORMATION: WHY LEADERSHIP MATTERS	9781636512273
LEADERSHIP ESSENTIALS	9781636510316
TIME MANAGEMENT ESSENTIALS	9781636511665

MODERN MARKETING AND SALES

CONSUMER BEHAVIOR ESSENTIALS	9781636513263
DIGITAL MARKETING ESSENTIALS	9781949395747
MARKETING MANAGEMENT ESSENTIALS	9781636511788
MARKET RESEARCH ESSENTIALS	9781636513744
MODERN ADVERTISING ESSENTIALS	9781636514857
SALES MANAGEMENT ESSENTIALS	9781636510743
SERVICES MARKETING ESSENTIALS	9781636511733
SOCIAL MEDIA MARKETING ESSENTIALS	9781636512181

*Also available in Hardback & Ebook formats

SELF-LEARNING MANAGEMENT SERIES

TITLE	PAPERBACK* ISBN
OPERATIONS MANAGEMENT	
AGILE ESSENTIALS	9781636510057
OPERATIONS & SUPPLY CHAIN MANAGEMENT ESSENTIALS	9781949395242
PRODUCT MANAGEMENT ESSENTIALS	9781636514796
PROJECT MANAGEMENT ESSENTIALS	9781636510712
STAKEHOLDER ENGAGEMENT ESSENTIALS	9781636511511

CURRENT AFFAIRS

DIGITAL SHOCK	9781636513805

*Also available in Hardback & Ebook formats

About the Author

Karthik is a visionary AI and Data Science leader with over 14 years of global experience building and scaling high-impact teams, platforms, and products across Fortune 100 companies and high-growth startups. A graduate of RV College of Engineering (Bangalore), he began his career at Mu Sigma as a Data Scientist in 2012.

Over the years, he has held leadership roles at Amazon, Mu Sigma, and Infogain, where he led strategic initiatives in Pricing Analytics, Customer Insights, and applied Generative AI. At Mu Sigma, he delivered large-scale data science solutions for Fortune 500 clients across industries. At Amazon, he tackled complex problems in Retail Pricing Analytics before leading the Alexa Knowledge AI team for the ANZ region. Karthik currently heads the Data Science vertical at Imarticus Learning (an EdTech firm), where he built the AI team from the ground up into a 50+ member organization.

His areas of specialization include Generative AI, Natural Language Processing (NLP), Machine Learning, Deep Learning, and building scalable Data Science Centers of Excellence (CoEs). A firm believer in the democratization of AI, he has helped organizations move from experimentation to enterprise-scale adoption through domain-driven, outcome-focused solutions.

A TEDx speaker and passionate storyteller, Karthik is recognized for demystifying complex data science topics for wider audiences through his writing, keynotes, and mentoring initiatives. He also serves as visiting faculty at institutions like IIM Lucknow and RVCE, where he mentors future leaders in AI. He remains committed to his core mission of AI literacy: bridging the gap between AI theory and business impact and preparing the next generation of AI-first thinkers and problem-solvers.

What Experts Say About This Book!

The author breaks down complex architectures into actionable insights, making it the perfect guide for both beginners and experts. A must-read for any professional working in the AI space looking to stay at the forefront of language model innovation.

– Mani Garlapati, Sr. Technical Program Manager, Google

This works as an excellent textbook, moving up the ladder of complexity of concepts necessary for anybody wanting to be an AI Engineer. The real-life examples at the end of each section are a must read.

– Kalpit Bhawalkar, Head of AI, Konverge AI

This book offers a systematic, instructor-ready framework that prepares students for meaningful AI use in professional settings. By grounding instruction in concrete examples, relevant conceptual distinctions, and applied decision-making frameworks, it avoids surface-level tool training and instead cultivates disciplined and principled thinking. The result is a learning experience that enables instructors to teach with intention and students to develop the practical, ethical competence required to embed AI responsibly into real business workflows.

– Karl R. LaPan, Director, UF Innovate | Accelerate The University of Florida

Some technology books feel like they are sprinting ahead, scattering jargon and assume you will keep up. This book doesn't. It slows down. It feels like it was written by someone who remembers what it is like to be curious before being confident.

There is no pressure to already understand AI. The author begins with the questions people usually ask–What is AI actually doing? Why does it matter? Where does human thinking end and machine learning begin? As a book lover, I appreciated that. I don't want to be impressed by complexity; I want to be invited to understand it. The explanations are

What Experts Say About This Book!

calm and clear. Concepts like machine learning and neural networks don't feel like paths you are guided along. You are never made to feel behind for not knowing something already. Instead, understanding builds quietly, until words that once felt intimidating start to feel familiar.

What stayed with me most is how human the book feels. AI isn't treated as a cold, distant force but as something shaped by human choices, data and values. The reminder running through the book is simple and lasting; AI reflects us. This isn't a book you rush through. I paused often, not from confusion, but from thought, noticing how deeply AI has already woven itself into daily life. That is what good books do, they follow you beyond the pages.

It is not a technical manual, and it won't turn you into an engineer or an expert. But if you want to understand before specializing, this book offers a steady, welcome foundation.

By the end, I didn't feel overwhelmed. I felt clearer, calmer and more curious. For a subject as vast and fast-moving as artificial intelligence, that is a quiet achievement.

– Himsekha Rai, NetGalley Reviewer

This book is good for those interested in AI regardless of their level of understanding.

I learned the history, how the concept was developed. I learned about the vast amounts of data required and about the various ways of organizing and interpreting data for productive use. I appreciate the practical examples, such as how email programs identify spam and how visual recognition programs work. As the programs advanced, examples of how programs recognize and interpret human speech are given and how generative programs can create text and images.

I also learned that the programs can make mistakes with a few examples given. The latest programs available are listed with suggestions for use

What Experts Say About This Book!

depending on what an individual wants to do with it. The ethical issues are also covered, giving examples of how the programs can be used to deceive people.

This is a very interesting book, much of it understandable by people not involved in programming.

– Joan Nienhuis, Reviewer, Book Reviews from an Avid Reader

I really enjoyed *Artificial Intelligence Essentials* You Always Wanted to Know because it finally made AI feel understandable instead of overwhelming. The explanations of machine learning, deep learning, NLP, and generative AI are clear, well structured, and written for people who are curious rather than those already having technical expertise, which I appreciated so much. I loved the way the book balances theory with real-world applications and practical examples, plus the summaries and quizzes actually helped reinforce what I was learning instead of feeling like a filler. It's the kind of guide that builds confidence as you read, and I finished it feeling informed, less intimidated, and genuinely excited about how AI fits into everyday life.

– Marta Petticoat, NetGalley Reviewer

A concise yet comprehensive guide covering the full spectrum of modern AI, from core ML/DL to the latest in GenAI and ethics. Highly recommended for building foundational literacy.

– Vinodh Balaraman, Co-founder & CEO, KolateAI Inc

Table of Contents

1 Introduction to Artificial Intelligence (AI) 1

1.1   Evolution of AI   2
1.2   Latest Trends in AI   8
1.3   AI Applications in Business   13
1.4   The Future of AI: A World of Possibilities   15
Chapter Summary   17
Quiz   18

2 Fundamentals of AI 21

2.1   Problem-Solving Journey Using AI   22
2.2   Supervised, Unsupervised, and Reinforcement Learning   27
2.3   AI Techniques   29
2.4   How to Build and Train an AI Model   33
Chapter Summary   37
Quiz   38

3 Machine Learning Techniques 41

3.1   Regression   44
3.2   Classification   51
3.3   Clustering   62
3.4   Key ML Algorithms and When to Use Them   66
3.5   Application of Machine Learning Algorithms   68
Chapter Summary   71
Quiz   72

4 Deep Learning   75

4.1   Introduction to Deep Learning (DL)   75
4.2   Neural Networks   80
4.3   Convolutional Neural Networks (CNNs)   91
4.4   Recurrent Neural Networks (RNNs)   98
4.5   Why is Deep Learning Becoming So Popular?   103
4.6   Challenges in Deep Learning   105
4.7   Application of Deep Learning Algorithms   106
Chapter Summary   111
Quiz   112

5 Natural Language Processing (NLP)   115

5.1   Fundamentals of NLP   117
5.2   NLP Project Pipeline   121
5.3   Transformers   130
5.4   Applications of NLP   134
Chapter Summary   142
Quiz   143

6 Computer Vision (CV)   147

6.1   Introduction and Evolution of Computer Vision   147
6.2   Key Components of Computer Vision   152
6.3   Object Detection   158
6.4   Image Generation: Generative Adversarial Networks
       (GANs)   164
6.5   Computer Vision Libraries   168
6.6   Applications of Computer Vision   169
Chapter Summary   174
Quiz   175

7   **Generative AI**   **179**

7.1   Introduction to Generative AI   179
7.2   Evolution of Generative AI   185
7.3   The Current Generative AI Landscape   193
7.4   Prompt Engineering   200
7.5   Large Language Models (LLMs)   207
7.6   Real-World Applications of GenAI   214
7.7   Conclusion   218
Chapter Summary   219

8   **Ethical AI**   **221**

8.1   Introduction to Ethical AI   221
8.2   Bias in AI   226
8.3   Transparency and Explainability   230
8.4   Governance in AI   233
8.5   Designing Ethical AI Systems   235
8.6   Conclusion   237
Chapter Summary   239

References   **240**

Glossary   **242**

Preface

We are at a defining moment in the evolution of business and technology where artificial intelligence is no longer a distant frontier, but a foundational force reshaping industries, decisions, and careers. Having spent 14 years solving real-world problems at the intersection of data, domain, and decision-making, from global corporations like Amazon to Mu Sigma, I've seen firsthand the transformative power of data science when applied with clarity and purpose.

This book is a product of those learnings. It distills insights gathered from building AI teams, designing platforms, leading strategic programs, and mentoring aspiring data scientists. But more importantly, it is rooted in a single belief: that AI doesn't need to be complex to be powerful. When grounded in business context, driven by curiosity, and executed with discipline, data science becomes less about algorithms and more about impact.

Whether you're a student, a working professional, or a business leader, this book is designed to help you think like a data scientist, not just code like one. It combines foundational concepts, real-world case studies, best practices, and emerging trends such as Generative AI to help you go beyond theory and into thoughtful application.

My hope is that this book becomes a trusted companion in your AI journey, sparking new ideas, challenging assumptions, and most importantly, enabling you to become a problem solver.

Here's to making AI work—practically, ethically, and impactfully!

Karthik
Bangalore, 2026

Introduction to the Book

You've heard the phrase: "Data is the new oil." But like crude oil, raw data in itself isn't valuable; it needs to be refined, contextualized, and converted into something useful. That refinery, in today's digital economy, is Artificial Intelligence (AI).

Whether it's Amazon optimizing millions of deliveries per day, Netflix keeping you glued to your screen, or banks preventing fraud in milliseconds, AI is the engine powering intelligent decision-making. And yet, for many, it remains a buzzword. Abstract. Reserved for a select few with PhDs or access to deep-pocketed R&D labs. This book challenges that idea.

AI is becoming democratized. With open-source tools, accessible learning platforms, and cloud-based infrastructure, anyone can now build AI systems that solve meaningful problems. But to do so effectively, you need more than algorithms. You need a way of thinking. This book is about that mindset.

You won't just find definitions of GenAI or NLP here; you'll learn how to actually put them to work. It's a guide to thinking like an AI practitioner, structuring fuzzy problems, blending business understanding with technical fluency, and using AI to create scalable, measurable impact.

You'll learn how to:

- Understand how AI-first companies approach problem framing
- Apply models not just to predict, but to prescribe and optimize

- Learn the fundamentals of moving from prototype to production-ready solutions
- Build the data, skills, and cultural foundations required for AI adoption

Drawing on over 14 years of real-world experience, building AI teams at Amazon and Mu Sigma, launching GenAI initiatives, and training thousands of learners globally, this book bridges the gap between theory and practice. Because in a world overflowing with data, the real value lies in how intelligently we use it.

Acknowledgments

This book is the result of years of learning, unlearning, experimenting, and building—across boardrooms, classrooms, and AI labs. It would not have been possible without the support, inspiration, and contributions of many individuals and institutions that have shaped my journey in the world of Artificial Intelligence.

First, I would like to thank the leadership at Vibrant Publishers for their trust and the creative freedom to shape this book.

To my professors at RV College of Engineering and St. Joseph's University (Bangalore)–thank you for teaching me the fundamentals and laying the groundwork upon which everything else was built.

To my mentors at Mu Sigma and Amazon - especially Mr. Dhiraj Rajaram (CEO and Founder of Mu Sigma) - thank you for setting the bar high and instilling a problem-solving mindset in me. The rigor and discipline I developed while scaling AI platforms in these organizations form the foundation of many ideas shared in this book.

I'm also deeply grateful to my peers in the AI community for their collaboration, insights, and inspiration. To my friends and family–thank you for your steady encouragement.

To my parents, Chandrakant Jannu and Chandrakala Jannu, who filled my childhood with stories of perseverance, lessons in integrity, and the quiet belief that knowledge is our greatest inheritance. Their tireless efforts in shaping my character and curiosity laid the foundation for everything that followed.

To my sister, Vibha SC, my lifelong partner in curiosity and courage, who celebrated every small win and turned every setback into our next adventure. Always my fiercest cheerleader, pushing me to do my best work. You've all been my constant anchor through this journey.

A special note of gratitude to Sri Sri Sachhidanand Jnaneshwar Bharati Mahaswami (Shree Jnaneshwari Peetha, Karki). Your guidance has been my spiritual compass, reminding me that true knowledge integrates intellect with wisdom and service.

Finally, to you, the reader—whether you're an aspiring AI practitioner, a business decision-maker, or simply curious: thank you for picking up this book. May it serve as a spark for your own learning, experimentation, and impact.

Who Can Benefit From This Book?

Aspiring Data Scientists

Students and recent graduates who are curious about how AI is applied in real-world business contexts will gain a practical understanding of Data Science fundamentals and industry use cases.

Experienced Professionals Transitioning into Data Science

Software developers, business analysts, and data analysts who are looking to pivot into Data Science roles will find this book valuable for understanding how AI and Data Science drive strategic decision-making in organizations.

AI Enthusiasts and Lifelong Learners

Individuals with a general interest in Artificial Intelligence will benefit from insights into the latest tools, algorithms, and technologies, along with real-world examples of how AI is shaping industries.

Business Leaders and Decision-Makers

Executives and managers seeking to leverage AI for competitive advantage will find accessible explanations of how AI can be applied to solve business problems and improve outcomes.

Educators and Trainers

Instructors and corporate trainers can use this book as a resource to introduce learners to the intersection of AI, business, and problem-solving through practical frameworks and case studies.

How to Use This Book?

This book is designed to be your practical companion on the journey to understanding Artificial Intelligence and its impact on the real world. Whether you are just getting started or seeking to deepen your knowledge, this book provides structured insights, simplified explanations, and real-life examples to help you connect theory with application.

Here are a few suggestions on how to get the most out of this book:

1. **If you are new to Artificial Intelligence:** Start from Chapter 1 and follow the sequence. The book is structured to build foundational understanding first, before moving into advanced topics.

2. **If you are an experienced tech or business professional:** You may skip directly to chapters that align with your goals– for instance, Chapters 3 and 4 can help you gain a deeper understanding of Machine Learning & Deep Learning.

3. **If you are exploring careers in AI or Data Science:** Use this book to understand the challenges, tools, techniques, and mindset needed to transition into an AI role.

4. **If you are simply curious about how AI impacts your world:** Chapters 7 and 8 explore the ethical, economic, and industry-wide implications of AI–a great place to understand how AI is shaping the future of business decision-making.

5. **Make it interactive:** Reflect on how the concepts relate to your work or interests. Think of your own examples. Try out simple projects or mini-experiments using the tools and approaches.

Introduction to Artificial Intelligence (AI)

Key Learning Objectives

- Explore the evolution of artificial intelligence (AI).
- Discover the latest trends in AI.
- Understand various business applications of AI.
- Gain insight into the future of AI.

Chapter 1 introduces artificial intelligence (AI), focusing on its evolution from early breakthroughs to the latest developments in the world of Generative AI. This chapter outlines various trends, technologies, and the way forward. It also showcases how various businesses today are using AI to improve their business metrics and performance. Lastly, the chapter explores the future landscape of artificial intelligence.

Have you ever wondered how we get recommendations on exactly what we like to see, hear, and wear in the world around us? How do brands and advertisers know about our likes and preferences? There's a friend, disguised as AI, making our lives more interesting with personalized suggestions.

In the 1950s, a famous question—*"Can machines think?"*—posed by Alan Turing (1950) in his seminal paper *"Computing Machinery and Intelligence"* sparked a profound discussion about the limits of intelligence.

Turing proposed that a computer could be considered capable of 'thinking' if it could engage in a conversation such that a human evaluator could not reliably distinguish it from a human. In his article, Turing also proposed the Turing Test as an investigation of machine intelligence. This test was created to evaluate whether a machine could exhibit intelligent behavior that is not different from that of a human (Turing, 1950).

It also created a shift in the discussion of machine intelligence from theoretical debates about whether machines can 'think' to a more practical assessment. He suggested that if a machine could converse well enough to fool a human evaluator, it could be considered intelligent.

A few years later, John McCarthy (1956) formally coined the term *Artificial Intelligence*, further fueling research aimed at surpassing human limitations.

1.1 Evolution of AI

At the Dartmouth Conference in 1956, a small group of scientists boldly posed the question, *"Could machines think like humans?"* This groundbreaking discussion was led by AI pioneers John McCarthy, Nathaniel Rochester, Marvin Minsky, and Claude Shannon (*McCarthy et al.*, 1955).

McCarthy, who is regarded as the father of artificial intelligence, first coined the phrase *"Artificial Intelligence,"* laying the foundation for the field and encouraging research into whether machines could learn, reason, and mimic human behavior (*McCarthy*, 1956).

Figure 1.1   A timeline of artificial intelligence

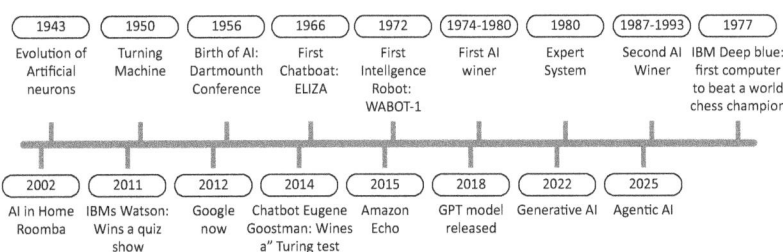

Source: Adapted from Javatpoint. (n.d.). History of artificial intelligence. https://www.javatpoint.com/history-of-artificial-intelligence

In the 1960s and 1970s, early AI systems attempted to learn, reason, and solve problems. While these systems demonstrated some capabilities, they also revealed the limitations of existing technology, highlighting the need for further research (*Nilsson*, 2010).

But by the 1980s, things were not going as planned. AI was a big topic. The "expert systems" that relied on human knowledge to make decisions were expensive, difficult to maintain, and ultimately failed to meet expectations (*Crevier*, 1993). As enthusiasm faded, AI entered a period known as the "AI winter" where research funding and interest declined significantly (*Hendler*, 2008).

Then, in the 2000s, the field of artificial intelligence saw a resurgence, driven by advances in big data and machine learning (*Domingos*, 2015).

Imagine a world where computers no longer just followed strict rules, but began to think for themselves—learning from the oceans of data available to them, like a musician learning to play an instrument for the first time.

In the beginning, each note sounds a bit off as they struggle to find the right rhythm. Sometimes hitting sour notes, but each mistake teaches them something new about timing, technique, and expression. They will quickly grow from a beginner into a talented artist, creating melodies that dive into deep emotions, captivate listeners, and give birth to entirely new musical masterpieces that spark inspiration and level up the imagination.

Figure 1.2 is an image generated by AI; it tells a story about how AI evolved with time. How amazing is that?

Figure 1.2 **An AI-generated image about the evolution of AI**

From mechanical calculators and advanced algorithms

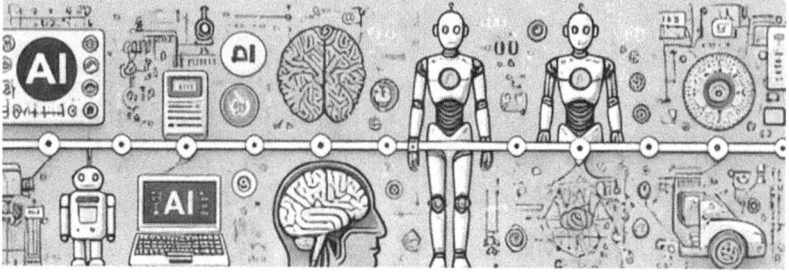

through neural networks and machine learning models

to deep learning algorithms that power self-driving cars

Source: Generated by AI

Using AI in this manner, we can turn our random thoughts into real pictures. This remarkable technology turns our imagination into advanced image recognition in our photo apps. It also forms the basis of technologies, such as voice assistants that understand human speech better and self-driving cars that navigate using detailed maps.

AI vs. Human Creativity: How Close Are We to Bridging the Gap

In the section below, there are two images. One is captured by a human photographer, whereas the other one is AI-generated using the Midjourney tool. Initial observation of the AI-generated image reveals that it very closely resembles reality, which showcases how far these AI models have reached when it comes to getting the intricate details, color, saturation, texture, lighting, etc. While AI can replicate it, it still lacks the depth, emotion, and the heuristic nature that humans bring to their creations. Despite that, AI-generated content (image, audio, video) is growing at a rapid pace. The real question is: When will it become impossible to tell the difference between a real image and one generated by AI?

Figure 1.3 **Image captured by a camera**

Source: Timothy Coleman's Instagram page, photograph shot in Kenya (2018)

Figure 1.4 A fictional reality composed by AI

Source: AI-generated image using Midjourney

Google Photos, for instance, was just another photo storage service that used basic algorithms to organize pictures. Users uploaded their photos, and the service sorted them into albums based on time and location. However, Google realized it could use the power of machine learning and vast amounts of data, and it was able to evolve into a smart system capable of detecting objects, identifying people, and even recognizing specific scenes or locations. So today, if you search for "food" in your Google Photos, it automatically fetches all the food-related pictures using AI-driven indexing.

Let's consider the example of YouTube, which started as a simple video-sharing platform where users could upload and watch videos. Initially, its recommendations were basic and random, like wandering through a maze without a map. As YouTube gained popularity, it utilized machine learning to analyze viewing patterns, considering factors like watch time, user interactions (likes, comments, shares), search history, and location data. By processing these data points, YouTube refined its recommendations based on individual preferences. Suddenly, viewers were treated to a personalized selection of content, and now many have become addicted to it. In most cases, one feels more connected to the virtual world than to human interaction, as machines show us exactly what we like to see, hear, or speak.

Deep learning is another subset of machine learning that uses neural networks to design and mimic the workings of the human brain. It also learns patterns and extracts insights from massive amounts of data.

Similarly, as speech recognition technology has advanced, we are actually living with invisible intelligence that has become an important part of our everyday lives. Alexa, Siri, or any other virtual assistant act as our invisible buddy, listening and talking to us, playing music, turning off lights, setting reminders, telling us jokes, or even telling us what to do next. Having worked on the natural language processing (NLP) & automatic speech recognition (ASR) aspects of Alexa firsthand during my stint at Amazon, I found the core idea of building intelligent systems very exciting.

NLP enables machines to understand and process human language, allowing virtual assistants to understand user commands or prompts. ASR, on the other hand, converts the spoken utterances into verbatim text, which is then useful for the system to recognize and respond more accurately. For example, when you ask Alexa, "What's the weather forecast for the day?", ASR transcribes this utterance into text, and the NLP identifies the intent to further process it and then fetches the weather forecast from relevant sources of data.

Humans are becoming more dependent on these invisible buddies, and there is no limit to this. Artificial intelligence is created by us, but it may get out of our hands if not used with ethical rules. It is already influencing the younger generation with a recommendation algorithm, reducing the need for real human interaction. Soon, the human mind may not be able to differentiate between reality and its own personalized mindset shaped by our invisible buddies.

1.2 Latest Trends in AI

As mentioned previously, this technology is growing without limits, making us increasingly reliant on it. But this raises an important question: *Can we truly trust AI if we don't fully understand its decisions?*

The "black-box" of AI remains a mystery as we don't quite know what lies within it, yet we follow it like a guiding North Star.

AI trends are rapidly evolving, and staying updated on these trends has become indispensable. Large language models (LLMs) are disrupting how machines can understand and generate human-like text with impressive creativity. Agentic AI is enabling more autonomous decision-making. Artificial general intelligence (AGI) aims to create machines that can reason and learn across domains, much like humans. At the same time, Explainable AI (XAI) is gaining importance as a means of ensuring transparency and trust in AI-driven decisions. Developing XAI tools reveals what's going on "under the hood."

These advancements are driving AI toward greater intelligence, autonomy, and accountability, and they are redefining its role in industries like healthcare, finance, and even art!

1.2.1 Large Language Models (LLMs)

Having an assistant who can text for you, take notes, sing, and set alarms sounds amazing, right? This is now possible thanks to LLMs like generative pre-trained transformer (GPT) and bidirectional encoder representations from transformers (BERT). Both are built on transformer architecture, which is revolutionizing how we interact with AI. LLMs like GPT and BERT can generate text that reads as if it were written by a human. Here are a few examples where these models are used in our day-to-day lives.

- They're used in chatbots, writing tools, and generating images, audio, and video, which makes AI helpful for daily tasks.

- These models are also used in customer service, information summarization, and enhancing the overall accessibility and usability of AI.

- They are boosting human productivity at work (especially in domains like software engineering, creative writing, art, etc.).

Key Trends

- **Real-time responses:** Cutting-edge AI technologies, such as OpenAI's Realtime API, now enable AI models to support real-time voice applications. They help the AI community build voice assistants and interactive applications more effectively than ever before.

- **Multimodal functions:** LLMs have evolved beyond text— they can now process and create images, audio, and video, broadening their applications in artistic domains and content creation.

- **Domain-focused models:** AI is becoming increasingly specialized, featuring models tailored for healthcare, life sciences, legal assessment, and finance. These sector-focused models provide more accurate and relevant insights.

- **Enhanced reasoning & planning:** LLMs are advancing to tackle intricate problem-solving and multi-stage reasoning, setting the stage for more independent AI agents in research and commercial uses.

- **Privacy and security improvements:** As concerns about data privacy grow, businesses are creating LLMs that function locally or emphasize user protection via differential privacy and encryption methods to enhance security.

1.2.2 Explainable AI (XAI)

Explainable AI, or XAI, is all about making AI decisions easier to understand. When users can see how an AI system arrives at its decisions, they're more likely to trust and feel comfortable using it. Tools like LIME (Local Interpretable Model-agnostic Explanations) and SHAP (SHapley Additive exPlanations) help explain what factors influence AI's decisions. LIME is a method that explains individual predictions by approximating the model locally with an interpretable one. Whereas, SHAP is a technique based on game theory that assigns each feature an importance value for a particular prediction, helping users understand the model outputs. For example, they can show whether income or credit history is the reason for a loan approval or rejection.

Big companies like Google and IBM are creating special tools to help explain AI, such as Google's Vertex Explainable AI and IBM's AI Explainability 360.

Key Trends

- **Transparency and trust:** As AI becomes more transparent, users and regulators are developing greater confidence in its outputs.

- **Setting standards:** Standardized frameworks ensure there is a common ground and common rules to compare different AI models fairly. Just like how we use benchmarks to compare smartphones or gadgets, AI requires standardized guidelines to assess models fairly. Standardized measurements promote uniformity, dependability, and confidence in these AI systems.

- **Real-time explanations:** AI is currently delivering prompt clarity in its choices, which is essential in areas such as healthcare (e.g., clarifying a diagnosis) and self-driving cars (e.g., justifying a vehicle's drop in acceleration).

- **Growing awareness:** More universities have incorporated XAI and are teaching XAI to prepare future AI experts. This ensures that AI is not a black-box, but rather something that we all can depend on and improve holistically.

1.2.3 Artificial General Intelligence (AGI)

AGI is a type of AI that, if created, would have the ability to think, learn, and solve problems across a wide range of tasks, much like a human. While most current AI systems are designed for narrow tasks (such as translation or image recognition), AGI would be capable of performing multiple complex functions with adaptability and general understanding. Right now, experts are trying to develop AGI by enabling systems to learn through practice, improve over time, and understand diverse types of information. AGI aims to be adaptable by being able to reason, learn new abilities, and adjust without direct programming.

However, AGI is not a reality yet. It remains an aspirational goal within the AI community, but if achieved, it could change many things, solve big problems, and make AI more powerful.

Key Trends

- **Ethics and safety:** AGI needs to be designed responsibly so that it benefits society. With the advancement of AGI, it is essential to establish responsible AI governance to avoid unforeseen repercussions and harmonize AI objectives with human principles.

- **Transformational capacity:** If properly advanced, AGI has the potential to transform industries, address worldwide issues (e.g., disease management, climate issues), and alter the dynamics between humans and machines.

Although AGI is still under development, it represents the next frontier in AI—one that may fundamentally alter the world.

1.2.4 Agentic AI

If LLMs are powerful assistants, then Agentic AI is the next step; AI that doesn't just respond, but acts.

Agentic AI refers to systems that can autonomously plan, decide, and execute tasks to achieve a goal. Instead of waiting for instructions at every step, these systems break down objectives into sub-tasks, choose the right tools, adapt to new information, and move toward outcomes with minimal human intervention.

In simple terms, traditional AI answers questions, while Agentic AI pursues goals. For example, imagine asking an AI not just to summarize market data, but to analyze competitors, identify pricing gaps, generate a strategy draft, and even simulate possible business outcomes. An agentic system can orchestrate multiple models, APIs, and workflows to complete that mission end-to-end.

This marks a fundamental shift—from AI as a tool to AI as a collaborator. However, with autonomy comes responsibility. As AI systems begin to act independently, questions around governance, control, accountability, and safety become even more critical. Organizations must define boundaries, escalation mechanisms, and oversight structures to ensure that autonomous systems align with business goals and ethical standards.

Key Trends

- **Goal-oriented systems:** AI agents are being designed to reason over long tasks, plan multi-step actions, and dynamically adjust strategies based on feedback.

- **Tool use and orchestration:** Agentic AI can connect with external tools, such as databases, software systems, APIs, enabling it to execute actions beyond text generation.

- **Human-in-the-loop governance:** Rather than full autonomy, most enterprise deployments combine AI agents with human oversight to ensure safety and alignment.

- **Enterprise workflow automation:** From finance reconciliation to customer onboarding, agent-based systems are beginning to transform operational efficiency.

- **Rise of multi-agent systems:** Instead of one large model doing everything, multiple specialized agents collaborate to solve complex business problems.

1.3 AI Applications in Business

AI is changing how businesses work across domains like retail, e-commerce, banking, finance, healthcare, manufacturing, life sciences, space, and others. Let's explore some of these prominent changes in the following section:

1.3.1 AI in Finance

Everything is inclining towards a paperless digital economy, and with such an advancement comes great risks. A lot of frauds take place, and people have become spendthrifts since the change from paper to digital currency. We need measures to keep a watch on that. AI models, particularly anomaly detection algorithms and predictive analytics, help identify suspicious transactions in real-time by analyzing patterns across massive datasets. For example, PayPal uses AI technology to detect fraudulent activities swiftly and accurately. AI is becoming essential in the financial sector—not just for security, but also for accessibility and personalization. As Bill Gates once noted: "With the rise of digital transactions, AI is essential for keeping our financial systems secure and making personalized financial tools accessible to everyone."

1.3.2 AI in Retail

AI is used to maximize sales by enabling recommendation systems, dynamic pricing, and inventory optimization. It helps create personalized shopping experiences, optimize supply chains, and drive operational efficiency for businesses. The use-cases are many, and it fulfills them by analyzing customer preferences and behavior to offer recommendations and dynamic pricing.

AI doesn't just influence what we buy—it shapes how we buy. From turning desires into real-time purchases to enhancing customer engagement through AI-powered chatbots (used by companies like Sephora and Domino's), AI is redefining the customer journey. Platforms like Salesforce Einstein AI help predict demand, optimize stock levels, and ensure supply matches consumer needs. This prevents both overproduction and shortages, creating a well-balanced inventory system.

Additionally, smart devices now allow customers to virtually try on outfits before purchasing, blending convenience with personalized shopping like never before.

1.3.3 AI in Healthcare

AI is transforming the healthcare sector by optimizing clinical trials and enabling personalized treatments as well as drug development through predictive modeling, medical image analysis, and robotic process automation (RPA). With the help of advanced predictive models, AI supports accurate disease diagnosis and facilitates personalized treatment for patients. It also automates routine administrative tasks, allowing healthcare providers to dedicate more time to direct patient care. AI plays a crucial role in drug discovery as well. AI algorithms accelerate research by simulations, thus significantly reducing the time and money required to develop a new drug.

1.3.4 AI in Space

Space exploration benefits tremendously from AI-driven autonomous navigation, satellite data processing, and anomaly detection. AI enables space scientists and astronauts to explore space like never before. AI-powered systems can operate in extreme environments, analyze vast amounts of data, and help uncover long-standing cosmic mysteries. Companies like Amazon Web Services (AWS), HawkEye 360, and Cognitive Space are actively working to harness AI's potential in space, making previously unattainable insights more accessible and actionable.

1.4 The Future of AI: A World of Possibilities

Sam Altman, the CEO of OpenAI, thinks that AGI could change how we work and bring fresh ideas that make life easier for everyone (Altman, 2025). Unlike traditional computers that operate with clear limitations, AGI would be a highly intelligent system capable of learning autonomously—adapting, evolving, and possibly even surpassing human intelligence.

Experts believe AGI might come in the next few years, and some say it could be here by 2027 or 2030. Currently, computers are designed to perform one task at a time. In the future, there is a possibility that it may perform parallel tasks with high accuracy.

OpenCog is one of the projects in this field that aims to combine multiple AI techniques—such as symbolic AI, machine learning, evolutionary algorithms, and probabilistic reasoning—to create a more powerful and adaptable system. By integrating these diverse approaches, OpenCog seeks to build an AI that can think, learn, and solve problems in a way that mimics human intelligence.

The rapid pace of AI development prompts us to ask profound questions: Will it go beyond just being a tool to help us and maybe start coming up with new ideas on its own? Or, will people always have the last word, with their own ideas and ways of thinking? As we stand on the edge of this new technological era, I find myself both fascinated and eager to adapt, ready to witness the breakthroughs that will uncover hidden mysteries and shape the future.

So, how will you harness the power of AI in your life? What role do you envision it playing in your future? Stay curious, and let's find out together in the next chapter.

Chapter Summary

- Artificial intelligence (AI) has become an integral part of daily life—powering personalized recommendations, voice assistants like Alexa and Siri, and many other smart technologies.

- The concept of AI dates back to the 1950s, with pioneers like Alan Turing and John McCarthy exploring whether machines could mimic human-like abilities.

- Following the dot-com era, AI experienced exponential growth, driven by advances in machine learning, the availability of large datasets, and the rise of cloud computing.

- A major focus for the future is the development of AGI—a form of AI capable of reasoning, learning, and adapting across multiple domains, much like a human.

- As AI continues to evolve rapidly, ensuring its responsible and ethical development is more critical than ever to harness its full potential while safeguarding societal well-being.

 **Quiz**

1. **Who first posed the question, "Can machines think?"**
   a. John McCarthy
   b. Marvin Minsky
   c. Alan Turing
   d. Claude Shannon

2. **What does the Turing test evaluate?**
   a. The memory capacity of machines
   b. The ability of a machine to mimic human intelligence
   c. The speed of computer processing
   d. The ethical implications of AI

3. **Who is popularly known as the father of artificial intelligence?**
   a. Nathaniel Rochester
   b. John McCarthy
   c. Marvin Minsky
   d. Alan Turing

4. **What term did John McCarthy introduce at the Dartmouth Conference in 1956?**
   a. Neural networks
   b. Machine learning
   c. Artificial intelligence
   d. Expert systems

5. **What was the primary reason for the "AI Winter" in the 1980s?**
   a. Lack of interest in AI research
   b. High costs and limited capabilities of expert systems
   c. Ethical concerns about AI
   d. Advances in robotics overshadowing AI

6. **Which technological advancement in the 2000s transformed AI?**
   a. Quantum computing
   b. Big data and machine learning
   c. Robotics and automation
   d. Blockchain technology

7. **What does deep learning use to mimic the human brain's functions?**
   a. Quantum processors
   b. Linear algorithms
   c. Neural networks
   d. Decision trees

8. **What major capability was enabled in Google Photos through AI?**
   a. Image indexing and recognition
   b. Real-time editing
   c. Enhanced storage capacity
   d. Real-time photo sharing

9. What subset of AI powers voice assistants like Alexa?
    a. Computer vision
    b. Predictive analytics
    c. Robotics
    d. Natural language processing (NLP)

10. Which tool is associated with Explainable AI (XAI)?
    a. TensorFlow
    b. Hadoop
    c. SHAP
    d. PyTorch

Answers

1 – c	2 – b	3 – b	4 – c	5 – b
6 – b	7 – c	8 – a	9 – d	10 – c

## CHAPTER 2

Fundamentals of AI

Key Learning Objectives

- Understand the end-to-end journey of problem-solving in AI.
- Explore various AI techniques and algorithms.
- Learn how AI models work and make predictions.
- Differentiate between supervised, unsupervised, and reinforcement learning.

In this chapter, we will delve deeper to understand the fundamentals of artificial intelligence, along with its problem-solving approach, core AI algorithms, and the process of creating AI models. AI is not just a technology, but a broad and evolving concept that includes various techniques designed to mimic human intelligence. To truly understand how AI works, we must examine its foundational elements, such as statistics and computing technologies, which play a critical role in shaping intelligent systems.

2.1 Problem-Solving Journey Using AI

AI is apt for tackling issues that are complicated for conventional methods, especially when we have huge amounts of data. From suggesting the next series on Netflix to enhancing delivery paths for logistic firms, AI's path begins with a thorough understanding of the problem statement. Once the problem is defined, which is the most important part of the journey, automatically, the remaining steps become easier to solve. Let's explore each of the steps in this journey below.

Figure 2.1 Six-step framework for solving problems using AI

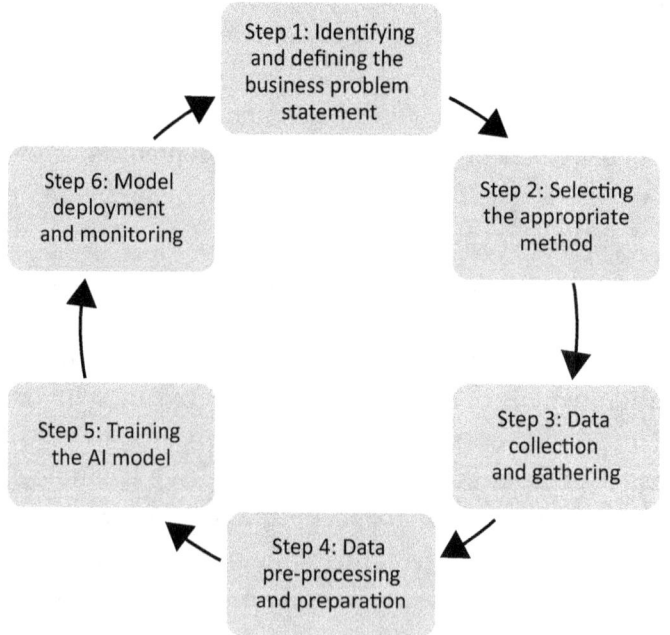

Step 1: Identifying and Defining the Business Problem Statement

Any effective AI solution begins by asking certain questions like:

- What issue are we addressing?
- Why is it important for the business?
- What type of information do we have?

The foundation of any AI solution lies in understanding the problem statement that you aim to solve. Thus, leveraging AI is not only about providing solutions, but also about asking the right questions.

Let's imagine a scenario where an online store observes that several customers add items to their carts but fail to finalize the transaction. This brings up two big questions: What causes users to leave or abandon their carts? And, what strategies can we implement to mitigate this problem?

The first step consists of converting this real-world problem into a concise, practical AI challenge. In our illustration, the problem can now be broken down as follows:

(a) Predict which users might abandon their carts

(b) Find suitable strategies to motivate them to finalize their purchase

A clear problem definition guarantees that the AI solution corresponds with business goals and user requirements.

Step 2: Selecting the Appropriate Method

AI is not a universal solution that fits every situation; sometimes, we must acknowledge that not every solution needs an AI solution. However, when an AI-driven approach is required, selecting the right method becomes important as part of the initial ideation phase.

In our example, to forecast cart abandonment, supervised learning could be the optimal choice. Supervised learning is a method that allows users to utilize labeled historical data. For instance, labelling users who left their carts versus those who completed purchases. On the other hand, identifying overall purchasing habits could be handled using unsupervised learning. This method detects patterns without the need for pre-existing labels.

For problems that require AI solutions, the crucial aspect is to align the AI algorithm with the specific problem statement. Choosing a suitable AI method depends on factors like the nature of the problem statement, the type of data that is currently available, and the desired outcome or results. While there are multiple options to choose from, it's important to ensure that we select the right AI algorithm for a particular business problem. Sometimes, it can get very iterative, and that is part and parcel of solving business concerns.

Step 3: Data Collection and Gathering

Data is the most essential element of AI. Step 3 revolves around the key functions of data, such as collecting relevant data, pre-processing it, and confirming that it accurately reflects the issue. In the previous example of an online store's cart abandonment, the dataset could include the following attributes:

- **Characteristics of users**, such as age, place of residence, and sex
- **Navigation habits**, such as duration on pages and number of clicks
- **Buying patterns**, such as products purchased and buying frequency

This phase includes gathering information, refining it to eliminate errors or discrepancies, and confirming that it correctly reflects the issue. For example, incomplete or skewed data may result in bad or poor predictions.

Step 4: Data Pre-Processing and Preparation

Once the raw data is gathered, it is essential to clean the data and carry out the necessary preprocessing steps in order to have a cleaner set of data. This is one of the most crucial steps involved before actually building the AI model. Data scientists often spend the majority of their time on data cleaning and preprocessing.

Data pre-processing includes data cleaning steps like removing duplicates and treating missing values. It also helps in identifying any outliers in the dataset.

Data preparation focuses on transforming data into a desired format to perform modeling. This includes steps like standardizing numerical features—scaling numbers so they have a consistent range or distribution—and encoding categorical variables, which means converting text labels (like "red" or "blue") into numbers so that machine learning models can use them. Sometimes, it also involves feature engineering, where new features are created as part of data preparation to help improve the model's performance.

Step 5: Training the AI Model

After the data is prepared and the algorithm is finalized, it's now time to create the AI model, the core engine of the AI system. Consider this as a process of instructing a learner. The model identifies patterns in the training data, similar to how a student learns through examples.

For instance, the model could discover that users who take less than two minutes to browse are more prone to leaving their cart. However, no AI model achieves perfection in the first attempt. Building an AI model is an iterative approach, and the model requires assessment and refinement until it operates effectively on new data. Through various iterations and experimentation, one can achieve enhanced model efficiency and accuracy.

Step 6: Model Deployment and Monitoring

Creating an AI model is merely the starting point; implementing it in a practical setting is among the toughest challenges in the AI domain. Deployment includes embedding the AI model into a current business system, ensuring scalability, enhancing inference speed, and managing real-time predictions. Deployment is not a one-time activity. After a model is deployed, it needs to adjust to changes in the real world. User patterns can change because of influences such as seasonal variations, economic conditions, or competitor behavior. Without ongoing supervision and updates, even the most advanced AI models may become obsolete.

While at Amazon, where I focused on pricing algorithms and strategies, I discovered that utilizing AI was merely the beginning. AI-driven pricing models needed constant assessment, retraining, and adjustments as competitor pricing, consumer demand, and market dynamics changed rapidly. We established automated pipelines that tracked model performance, identified drift, and initiated updates when necessary. The aim was not to create a flawless model, but to improve, enhance, and reliably provide business value at scale.

2.2 Supervised, Unsupervised, and Reinforcement Learning

AI learning paradigms define how machines are trained. Let's explore the three primary approaches to training: supervised learning, unsupervised learning, and reinforcement learning. We will examine each of these further, along with examples.

Figure 2.2	Types of machine learning paradigms

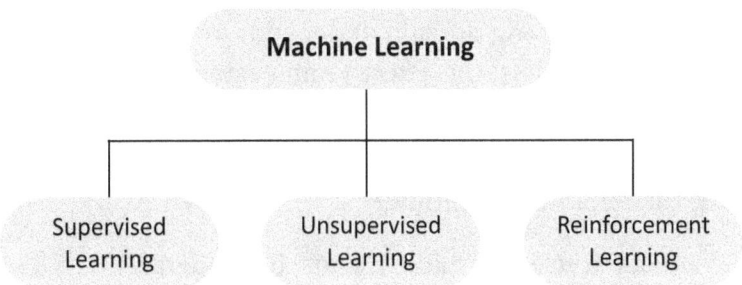

2.2.1 Supervised Learning

The supervised learning approach is similar to instructing a kid using flashcards. You give annotated examples (input and accurate output), and the model learns to associate the two. Let's take historic sales data as input, and the result is the forecasted sales as output. Supervised learning excels in areas such as fraud detection and predictive analysis across domains.

In supervised learning, labeled data becomes very important. The training dataset would have input and output pairs. For example, a dataset of emails labeled as "Spam" or "Not spam."

The most common supervised learning algorithms are linear regression, logistic regression, random forest, support vector machines (SVM), and neural networks. Some common challenges in supervised learning include overfitting (when the model learns too much from the training data), underfitting (when the model doesn't learn enough), and bias-variance tradeoff, which is about finding the right model complexity that minimizes both bias (error due to overly simplistic models) and variance (error due to overly complex models).

In short, supervised learning is a widely used approach in the machine learning domain. It depends on labeled data to train the ML models. It is effective and can help improve the model's accuracy.

2.2.2 Unsupervised Learning

In unsupervised learning, the machine operates independently to unearth patterns within data, without any predefined labels. It doesn't depend on any input-output pairs but just the underlying pattern of data. Typical use cases are segmenting customers and identifying fraudulent transactions by detecting anomalies.

For example, unsupervised algorithms can categorize customers into separate groups based on buying patterns or reveal hidden topics in textual data. Common unsupervised learning algorithms include clustering, association rules, and anomaly detection. These techniques improve recommendation systems and offer crucial insights in market analysis, network security, and bioinformatics by uncovering hidden patterns that promote data-driven decision-making.

2.2.3 Reinforcement Learning

Reinforcement learning works in changing environments where actions result in outcomes. The system acquires knowledge by earning rewards or facing penalties depending on its actions. This approach is commonly utilized in robotics, autonomous vehicles, gaming, healthcare, and financial trading. Unlike supervised learning, where the actual answer is provided in the training set, reinforcement learning works by learning from the consequences of actions to increase the rewards with time.

Reinforcement learning involves continuous experimentation with trial and error in an agentic framework, where an agent eventually learns to make better, insightful decisions by maximizing rewards over time.

2.3 AI Techniques

The foundation of artificial intelligence systems consists of various techniques, but their success relies on the quality of their design and application in addressing issues. Techniques like regression and classification allow machines to examine patterns, derive conclusions, and make informed decisions by utilizing historical data. These AI techniques form the basis for addressing intricate business challenges that frequently resemble human decision-making processes.

This section discusses several commonly used AI techniques within today's problem-solving environment, along with real-world applications.

2.3.1 Regression

Regression is used to predict continuous outcomes, such as forecasting sales revenue or predicting house prices.

Techniques like linear regression help establish relationships between variables, while advanced methods like polynomial regression capture more complex trends. Regression is a supervised learning method employed to forecast continuous results. It creates a connection between dependent and independent variables. The model determines the optimal line or curve that best fits the data points. Its main objective is to reduce the discrepancy between projected and actual values.

Regression aids in predicting trends like real estate costs or stock prices. It is essential in both statistics and machine learning for analyzing trends and making predictions. Linear regression and random forest regression are some of the most popular regression-based algorithms.

2.3.2 Classification

Classification focuses on categorizing data into predefined groups, which could be binary or more. It finds extensive use in areas such as spam identification, image recognition, and medical diagnosis. Classification is a supervised learning approach designed to sort data into distinct categories. It learns from annotated instances to differentiate between various categories. The procedure entails forecasting a category or class label for new data entries.

Logistic regression, decision trees, and support vector machines are commonly used algorithms for classification. In most real-world industry problems, the issue is either a regression or a classification problem. The effectiveness of the model is usually assessed using metrics such as accuracy, precision, and recall.

Figure 2.3   A visual representation of the classification technique

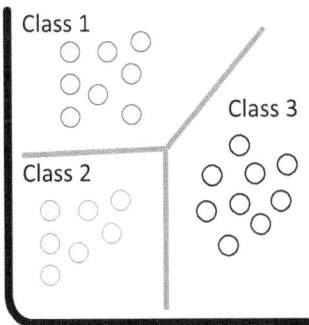

Source: Adapted from Bhardwaj, A. (2022). What are classification models in supervised learning. Medium. https://iaviral.medium.com/classification-models-cb4ba55c6f4d

2.3.3 Neural Networks

Inspired by the way human brains handle and process information, neural networks are a fundamental concept in the world of artificial intelligence. They are made up of layers of linked nodes called neurons, with each one carrying out minor calculations. When integrated and combined, these layers identify patterns in data, similar to how our brain detects faces or understands speech or video. Neural networks power facial recognition technologies used in security systems or smartphone access. The greater the depth of the network (i.e., the more layers it has), the more effectively it can detect intricate relationships. This ability to model intricate dependencies is what gives deep learning, an advanced branch of neural networks, its remarkable power.

Convolutional neural networks (CNNs), recurrent neural networks (RNNs), and long short-term memory (LSTM) are the most popular neural networks.

2.3.4 Clustering Algorithms

Clustering is similar to arranging your wardrobe. You categorize items into shirts, pants, shoes, etc., according to their resemblances. In artificial intelligence, clustering algorithms categorize data points without predefined labels.

One major application of clustering is customer segmentation. Companies use clustering techniques to divide their customers into different segments, such as price-sensitive shoppers or high-end buyers. This segmentation allows businesses to tailor their marketing strategies to better meet the needs and preferences of each group.

Another important use of clustering is in anomaly detection. In cybersecurity, for example, clustering can help identify unusual patterns or behaviors that may indicate a potential hacking attempt. Similarly, in the BFSI (Banking, Financial Services, and Insurance) sector, clustering is often used to detect fraudulent transactions by spotting data points that deviate from the norm.

K-means, agglomerative hierarchical clustering, and DBSCAN (density-based spatial clustering of applications with noise) are the most popular clustering algorithms.

2.3.5 Reinforcement Learning

Consider how you would teach a dog to retrieve a ball. Each time the dog retrieves correctly, it receives a reward (a treat). If it fails to do so, there won't be a reward. With time, the dog discovers the actions that lead to rewards. This algorithm also functions similarly, enabling artificial intelligence to discover the best actions through interactions with an environment and obtaining feedback.

An example of the same can be seen in supply chain optimization, which is utilized by companies to enhance warehouse capabilities. It keeps a check on inventory management and monitors deliveries in real time.

2.3.6 Natural Language Processing (NLP)

NLP algorithms are prominently used to solve text-based problems. They understand, analyze, and produce human language. Recent advancements, such as transformers, have enabled AI to accomplish tasks that previously seemed impossible. It can help in summarizing documents, writing essays, or even engaging in a human-like conversational setup. Applications such as Siri, Alexa, and AI support bots utilize NLP to answer user questions. NLP can also be used in content generation. Tools like ChatGPT produce text, from basic summaries to imaginative stories, with remarkable precision as well as humor.

BERT (bidirectional encoder representations from transformers), GPT (generative pre-trained transformer), and RRNs (recurrent neural networks) are the most popular algorithms used in NLP.

2.4 How to Build and Train an AI Model

Creating an AI model resembles training a sports competitor; it demands discipline, assessment, and refinement as discussed in Section 2.1 earlier. It can be a highly iterative and experimental process. Let's break it down and understand the same in simple steps listed below.

Remember, these steps may require multiple iterations before a robust ML/AI model is built and finalized.

| Figure 2.4 | Core stages of AI model creation |

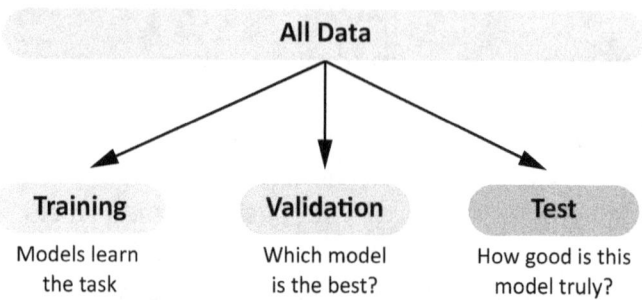

Training: This is where the model acquires knowledge by going through examples paired with their accurate responses. This is the learning phase where the model is exposed to labeled data. It analyzes patterns and relationships between input features and outputs to make accurate predictions. For example, in a spam detection system, the model processes thousands of emails labeled as "spam" or "not spam" to learn distinguishing features.

Validation: An independent collection of examples is utilized during training to evaluate the model's advancement and adjust its parameters. Validation ensures that the model generalizes well to unseen data and is not just memorizing training examples. A separate dataset, which is called the validation set, is used during training to fine-tune hyperparameters and prevent overfitting.

Testing: Once training is complete, the model undergoes evaluation on an entirely different collection of examples. Testing demonstrates the model's effectiveness on new, real-world data it hasn't encountered before. This step also provides a real-world assessment of its performance, measuring metrics like accuracy, precision, recall, and F1-score.

Continuous improvement: AI models require ongoing refinement. As new data becomes available, retraining the model helps adapt to changing trends and improve accuracy. Regular monitoring ensures that the model continues to deliver optimal results in dynamic environments.

The following are a few essential performance metrics to monitor any AI model's improvement:

(a) Accuracy: The frequency at which the model produces accurate predictions

(b) Precision and recall: Management of false alarms and missed detections

Points to Remember

- Precision measures how many of the predicted positive cases were actually positive (useful for reducing false alarms).

- Recall (or sensitivity) measures how many of the actual positive cases were correctly identified (useful for minimizing missed detections).

(c) F1 score: An all-encompassing measure that merges both precision and recall in a single metric

EXAMPLE

Example Scenario: AI-Powered Customer Support Chatbot

Imagine an e-commerce company developing an AI chatbot to handle customer queries. The training process involves:

- Feeding the chatbot with historical customer conversations *(training)*.

- Evaluating responses against unseen queries to fine-tune the model *(validation)*.

- Deploying the chatbot and testing its real-time performance *(testing)*.

- Refining responses based on new customer interactions *(continuous improvement)*.

This structured approach ensures that AI models remain relevant, accurate, and aligned with business goals.

As we conclude this chapter, keep in mind the core business problem while building an AI model, and also the purpose for which you're building the model. Once you experiment with different models, it becomes very important to narrow them down and finalize on the champion model, which will then be finalized for production level. So, always ensure that you are building an AI model that is aligned with the business requirements to get maximum value out of the solution.

Chapter Summary

- The AI problem-solving journey begins with clearly identifying and defining a business problem. The process involves selecting the appropriate AI method, collecting and preparing data, training the model, and continuously monitoring its performance after deployment.

- AI models learn through three main paradigms: supervised learning, unsupervised learning, and reinforcement learning.

- Various techniques such as regression, classification, clustering, neural networks, reinforcement learning, and NLP are employed depending on the problem type and data.

- The AI model development lifecycle includes training, validation, testing, and continuous improvement.

- The effectiveness of any AI model depends on how well it aligns with business objectives.

Quiz

1. **What is the first step in solving a problem using AI?**

   a. Collecting data

   b. Building the AI model

   c. Identifying and defining the business problem

   d. Monitoring the model

2. **Why is data considered the most essential element of AI?**

   a. It ensures predictions are always accurate.

   b. It provides the foundation for training AI models.

   c. It prevents algorithm bias.

   d. It automates the AI process.

3. **What type of learning is used to forecast cart abandonment using labeled historical data?**

   a. Supervised learning

   b. Unsupervised learning

   c. Reinforcement learning

   d. Clustering

4. **Which of the following is a use case for decision trees?**

   a. Detecting spam emails

   b. Predicting customer purchase behavior

   c. Recognizing faces in images

   d. Generating creative content

5. **What does reinforcement learning rely on to train models?**
   a. Supervised datasets
   b. Feedback through rewards and penalties
   c. Unlabeled data
   d. Random guessing

6. **What is the role of preprocessing in AI?**
   a. Visualizing the data
   b. Eliminating errors and preparing data for modeling
   c. Building the AI model
   d. Selecting an algorithm

7. **Which algorithm mimics the way the human brain works?**
   a. Decision trees
   b. Reinforcement learning
   c. Clustering algorithms
   d. Neural networks

8. **What is a common application of clustering algorithms?**
   a. Forecasting
   b. Customer segmentation
   c. Predicting sales data
   d. Natural language processing

9. **What is the key outcome of model validation?**
   a. Ensuring the model performs well in real-world scenarios
   b. Building a better model
   c. Collecting data
   d. Selecting a learning paradigm

10. **Which metric combines precision and recall?**

   a. Accuracy
   b. F1 score
   c. Sensitivity
   d. Specificity

Answers

1 – c	2 – b	3 – a	4 – b	5 – b
6 – b	7 – d	8 – b	9 – a	10 – b

CHAPTER 3

Machine Learning Techniques

Key Learning Objectives

- Explore the top machine learning (ML) algorithms: regression, classification, and clustering.
- Understand when and where to use the machine learning algorithms.
- Discover practical business applications of ML algorithms.

In this chapter, we will explore various machine learning algorithms and their functionalities in detail. While ML is a vast field, we'll focus on the core essentials for understanding AI-driven solutions. Not only will you learn how these algorithms work, but you will also see how they are applied to solve real-world business problems across various domains. By the end of this chapter, you will be prepared to experiment with ML algorithms yourself.

Machine learning is a key sub-branch of artificial intelligence. It enables machines to learn from data and make informed decisions. These algorithms identify patterns in data and help predict similar or new sets of data. The practical applicability of ML is tremendous and can be found across different industries, including image and speech recognition, natural language processing (NLP), recommendation systems, fraud detection, and churn analysis, among others.

Machine learning includes a variety of algorithms, each suited to different types of use cases. The illustration below shows various techniques grouped into categories such as regression, classification, clustering, dimensionality reduction, neural networks, ensemble methods, and Bayesian approaches.

Some commonly used algorithms include:
- Linear and logistic regression for forecasting models
- Decision trees and ensemble techniques such as random forest and gradient boosting for classification tasks
- Principal component analysis (PCA) for dimensionality reduction
- Deep learning architectures like convolutional neural networks (CNNs) and deep belief networks (DBNs) for handling high-dimensional data such as images and text

Figure 3.1 Machine learning algorithms

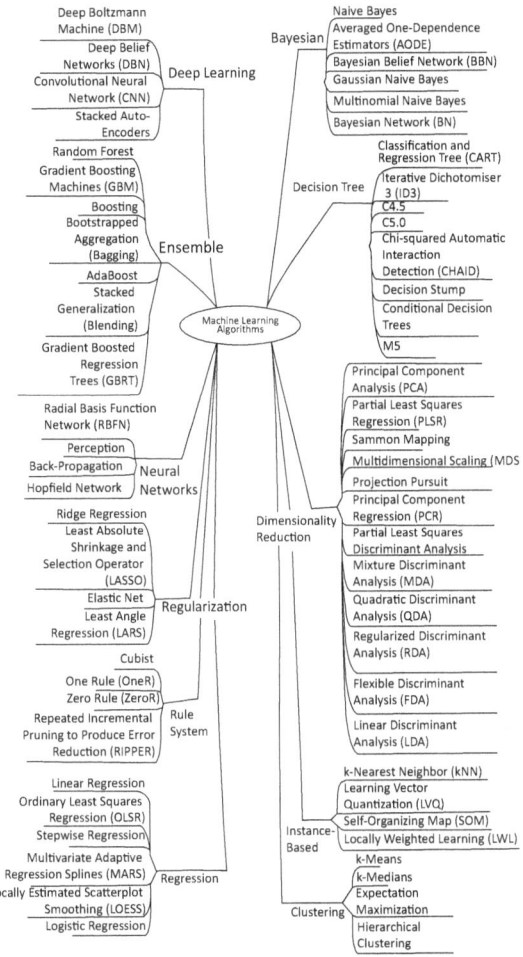

Source: Khan, M. A., Algarni, A. D., Ramesh, K., & Nayak, R. S. (2021). Applications of machine learning algorithms in molecular diagnostics. Expert Review of Molecular Diagnostics, 21(4), 403–417. https://doi.org/10.1080/14737167.2021.1886083

The core of ML revolves around three key techniques: regression, classification, and clustering. The majority of business problems are either regression or classification problems. Let's take a closer look at each of these techniques.

3.1 Regression

Throughout my years of experience with large-scale data, I have discovered that regression is among the most adaptable techniques available to any data scientist. Think about regression as sketching a line among dispersed points. It assists us in understanding the connections between variables and makes forecasts, like predicting future sales or estimating house prices.

Figure 3.2 **A visual representation of linear regression**

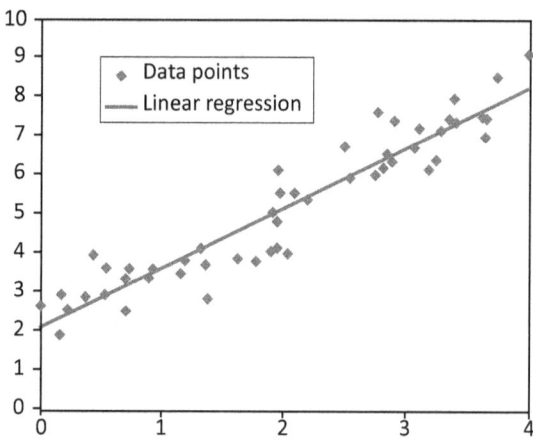

The most basic type, linear regression, assumes a straight-line relationship between variables. For example, when estimating property prices, we could take into account elements such as square footage, bedroom count, and location. Nonetheless, actual relationships in the real world aren't always straightforward. This is where advanced regression methods become relevant. Polynomial regression can model curved relationships, whereas multiple regression deals with several input variables at the same time. While at Amazon, we often employed these methods for demand prediction, aiding in the optimization of inventory quantities across different warehouses.

Here are some key considerations when selecting a regression method:

- Simple linear regression is effective when a distinct linear connection exists between variables.
- Multiple linear regression is suitable when various variables affect the result.
- Polynomial regression is essential when relationships exhibit distinct curvature.

Simple linear regression is among the most straightforward and commonly utilized algorithms in machine learning. It is utilized for forecasting a continuous numerical value by analyzing the connection between one or more input variables (features) and an output variable (target).

Linear regression assumes that there is a **linear relationship** between the independent variables (**X**) and the dependent variable (**Y**). This relationship can be expressed with a straight-line equation:

$$y = \beta_0 + \beta_1 X + \varepsilon$$

Where:

y - Dependent variable

x - Independent variable

β_1 - Regression coefficient

ε - Error of the estimate

β_0 - Intercept, the value of y when x is 0

3.1.1 Assumptions in Linear Regression

Let's try to understand the key assumptions of linear regression. These are important to ensure that the model generates valid and reliable results.

Linearity

This is the fundamental assumption in linear regression. The connection between our predictors (independent variables) and the result (dependent variable) ought to display a linear trend. Consider graphing house prices in relation to square footage and assuming a linear relationship between them. If the plotted points approximately align along a straight line, this assumption is valid. In reality, achieving perfect linearity is uncommon, yet we seek fairly linear relationships.

Independence of Observations

Every data point must be independent of the others. Consider forecasting monthly sales—if the sales from one month significantly impact those of the following month, this premise is compromised. This holds significant importance in time series data. While I was examining retail data, we frequently had to revise our models to reflect seasonal dependencies.

Homoscedasticity

This indicates that the difference between predicted and actual values must remain consistent. For example, when predicting house prices—whether for a small home or a large luxury estate—the spread of prediction errors should be roughly the same. If the spread of errors increases as house size increases, we encounter heteroscedasticity (where the spread of errors changes across different values of the input, instead of staying constant), potentially resulting in unreliable predictions.

Standard Distribution of Mistakes

The residuals (errors) are expected to conform to a normal distribution. If we graph all the variances between our predicted values and real values, they ought to create a bell-shaped curve. This assumption is especially crucial when we aim to conduct statistical tests on our regression outcomes or establish confidence intervals.

No Multicollinearity

Our predictor variables must not be overly correlated with one another. For example, when predicting home prices based on square footage and room count, these factors could be too interconnected, complicating the model's ability to assess the distinct impact of each variable.

Adequate Sample Size

We require a sufficient number of data points to assess the connections in our model accurately. The more data we have, the better the model can learn patterns. Having larger data also helps make predictions more reliable. This will guarantee that our model can identify genuine patterns in the data instead of merely capturing noise.

3.1.2 Performance Metrics for Regression

To evaluate how well a regression model is performing, we use a set of performance metrics that measure the accuracy of its predictions. These assist us in grasping how much the model's predictions differ from the real results, and how effectively it identifies the fundamental patterns in data.

Mean Absolute Error (MAE)

It calculates the average absolute differences between the predicted and actual values. It helps us understand that, on average, the model's predictions deviate from the actual values.

Formula:

$$\text{MAE} = \frac{1}{n}\sum_{i=1}^{n}\left|y_i - \hat{y}_i\right|$$

Where:

y_i = actual value

$\hat{y}_i$ = predicted value

n = number of observations

Mean Squared Error (MSE) and Root Mean Squared Error (RMSE)

MSE is used to quantify the average squared difference (or its square root) between predictions and actual values, emphasizing larger errors. These metrics penalize larger errors more than MAE.

$$\text{MSE} = \frac{1}{n}\sum_{i=1}^{n}\left(y_i - \hat{y}_i\right)^2$$

$$\text{RMSE} = \sqrt{\text{MSE}} = \sqrt{\frac{1}{n}\sum_{i=1}^{n}\left(y_i - \hat{y}_i\right)^2}$$

R-squared (Coefficient of Determination)

R^2 is the key output metric to consider for regression. It indicates the proportion of variance in the target variable that the model explains. It ranges from 0 to 1, where 1 means ideal prediction and 0 means the model is not doing any better than predicting the mean value.

Formula:

$$R^2 = 1 - \frac{SS_{res}}{SS_{tot}}$$

Where:

$SS_{res} = \sum\left(y_i - \hat{y}_i\right)^2$ (residual sum of squares)

$SS_{tot} = \sum\left(y_i - \bar{y}\right)^2$ (total sum of squares)

$\bar{y} = $ mean of actual values

Adjusted R-squared

This is a revised version of R-squared that adjusts for the number of predictors, providing a slightly more accurate measure when multiple features are present. It is particularly useful when comparing models with different numbers of variables, as it penalizes unnecessary complexity.

Formula:

$$\text{Adjusted } R^2 = 1 - \left(\frac{\left(1 - R^2\right)\left(n - 1\right)}{n - k - 1} \right)$$

Where:

n = number of observation

k = number of predictors

3.1.3 Linear Regression in Python

Here's a simple implementation of linear regression in Python with the help of scikit-learn.

Import the Necessary Libraries

Let's start by importing the required libraries:

Reference links: NumPy: https://numpy.org/, Matplotlib: https://matplotlib.org/, scikit-learn: https://scikit-learn.org/

```
import numpy as np
import matplotlib.pyplot as plt
from sklearn.linear_model import LinearRegression
```

Create or Import a Dataset

Now that all the libraries are loaded, let's create a simple dataset to build a linear regression model.

```
# X: Years of experience
# y: Salary in thousands
X = np.array([1, 3, 5, 7, 9]).reshape(- 1, 1)
y = np.array([30, 50, 70, 85, 90])
```

Train the Model

Let's train the model and then generate predictions.

```
model = LinearRegression()
model.fit(X, y)
predicted = model.predict(X)
print("Predicted salaries:", predicted)
print("Slope (coefficient):", model.coef_[0])
print("Intercept:", model.intercept_)
```

Plot the Regression Line

In this case, the red line in the plot is the model's prediction, and it shows how salary increases with experience.

```
plt.scatter(X, y, color='blue', label='Actual')
plt.plot(X, predicted, color='red', label='Predicted
(Regression Line)')
plt.xlabel('Years of Experience')
plt.ylabel('Salary (in thousands)')
plt.title('Linear Regression')
plt.legend()
plt.show()
```

Here is what the output would look like:

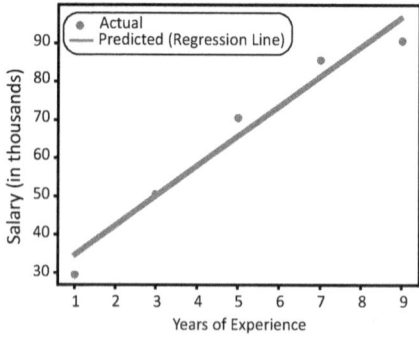

3.2 Classification

Classification is a fundamental technique in machine learning that is used to predict which category or class a given data point belongs to. Unlike regression, which forecasts continuous values, classification categorizes items into designated categories or classes. It's more about categorizing labels such as "Spam" or "Not Spam," "Healthy" or "Unhealthy," and so on. During my career, I've applied classification algorithms for multiple applications, ranging from identifying fraudulent transactions to incorrect product pricing.

Figure 3.3 A visual representation of classification

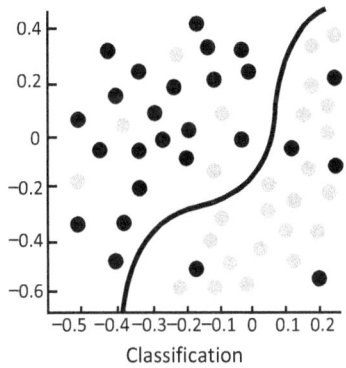

Classification

Source: Arya, N. (2022, April 4). Logistic Regression for Classification. KDnuggets. https://www.kdnuggets.com/2022/04/logistic-regression-classification.html

The selection of a classification algorithm largely depends on the specific application. For example, logistic regression, contrary to what its name suggests, is a classification algorithm that performs effectively for binary classification problems. Decision trees provide results that are easy to interpret, making them ideal for scenarios where one must clarify the model's choices to non-technical stakeholders.

Similarly, support vector machines (SVM) are highly effective at managing intricate classification issues. They do this by identifying the best boundaries that separate various classes. Random forest, which aggregates various decision trees, typically yields strong results and is more resistant to overfitting. In my experience with retail analytics, we relied heavily on random forests for predicting customer churn, as they managed our combination of categorical and numerical data exceptionally well.

Let's get an overview of each classification algorithm discussed above:

Logistic Regression

Logistic regression, a linear model primarily used for binary classification (e.g., Yes/No, True/False, High/Low), calculates the likelihood that a data point belongs to a specific class using the logistic (sigmoid) function. It's straightforward, quick, and easy to interpret, but it assumes a linear relationship between the input features and the log-odds of the result. It estimates the probability that a given input belongs to a particular class using the sigmoid function:

$$P(y = 1 \mid X) = \frac{1}{1 + e^{-(\beta_0 + \beta_1 X_1 + \cdots + \beta_n X_n)}}$$

Note: While logistic regression is commonly associated with binary classification, it can also be extended to multi-class problems.

How logistic regression works: Let's try to understand with an example.

The graph below helps us understand how logistic regression predicts whether a person will buy health insurance based on their age. The X-axis here represents age in years, and the Y-axis represents the probability of purchasing health insurance.

Figure 3.4 Logistic regression model for health insurance purchase

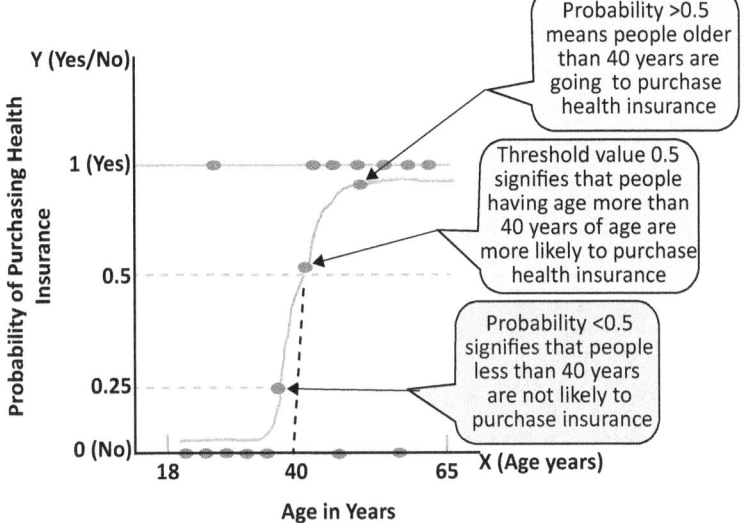

People under the age of 40 generally have a low predicted probability (< 0.5), meaning they are not likely to purchase insurance. In contrast, people over the age of 40 tend to have a higher predicted probability (> 0.5), indicating they are more likely to purchase insurance.

Threshold = 0.5: This is the decision boundary. If the model predicts a probability > 0.5, it classifies the person as someone who will purchase insurance (Yes = 1). Otherwise, it classifies them as No = 0.

Now that we have a general understanding of how logistic regression works, let's look at some key assumptions required for implementing it:

- The dependent variable is binary or dichotomous
- There is little or no multicollinearity between predictor variables
- There is a linear relationship between independent variables and log odds

- A sufficiently large sample size is required
- There are no extreme outliers
- Observations should be independent

Decision Trees

Decision trees divide the dataset into branches based on feature thresholds, forming a tree-like structure that results in a decision outcome at each leaf node. They are easy to understand and can represent complex, non-linear relationships. However, they tend to overfit the training data unless regulated through pruning or used alongside other methods.

Each node in a decision tree represents a decision rule, while each leaf node corresponds to a class label. Although decision trees are visually intuitive and effective at capturing intricate patterns, overfitting is a common issue if proper regularization is not applied.

Figure 3.5 **Structure of a decision tree**

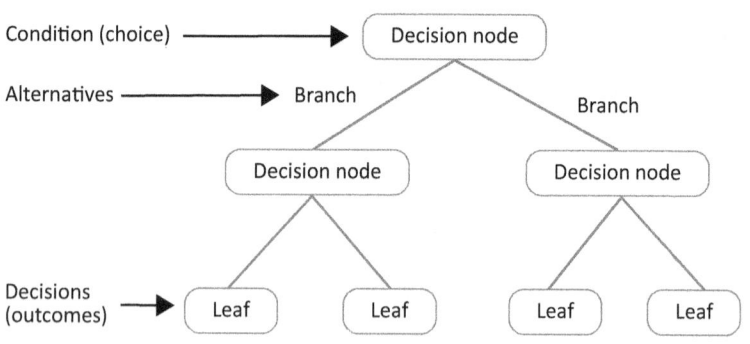

Gini impurity is a common criterion that is used in decision trees for splitting. It shows how often a randomly chosen item from a group would be incorrectly labeled, based on the mix of classes in that group. The goal is to make splits that reduce impurity, so that each group becomes as "pure" (mostly one class) as possible. The Gini index is always between 0 and 1, regardless of the number of classes.

Let's try to understand decision trees with a simple example:

Imagine you are a sports event management company that would like to decide whether to host a cricket match between India and England based on weather conditions. The dataset has attributes like Outlook, Temperature, Humidity, Wind, and a decision variable indicating whether the match was played or not in the past. Using this data, we will build a decision tree model to predict whether a match should be conducted or postponed based on the current weather conditions.

Let's say we want to predict the outcome for a new day with the following conditions:

Outlook: Rainy

Temperature: Mild

Humidity: High

Windy: True

The decision tree evaluates the conditions in a top-down method:

1. **Start at the root node, say it splits first on Outlook.**
   Is Outlook = Rainy? → Yes → move to the "Rainy" branch.

2. **The next node may split on Temperature**
   Is Temperature = Mild? → Yes → move to the "Mild" branch.

3. **The next node may split on Humidity.**
   Is Humidity = High? → Yes → move to the "High" branch.

4. **This leads to a leaf node that holds the final decision based on past data, e.g., "Don't Play."**

This path represents one complete decision-making route (or "pass") through the tree.

Figure 3.6 Making predictions using historical weather data

Outlook	Temperature	Humidity	Windy	Play
sunny	hot	high	false	no
sunny	hot	high	true	no
overcast	hot	high	false	yes
rainy	mild	high	false	yes
rainy	cool	normal	false	yes
rainy	cool	normal	true	no
overcast	cool	normal	true	yes
sunny	mild	high	false	no
sunny	cool	normal	false	yes
rainy	mild	normal	false	yes
sunny	mild	normal	true	yes
overcast	mild	high	true	yes
overcast	hot	normal	false	yes
rainy	mild	high	true	no

Figure 3.7 Decision tree output

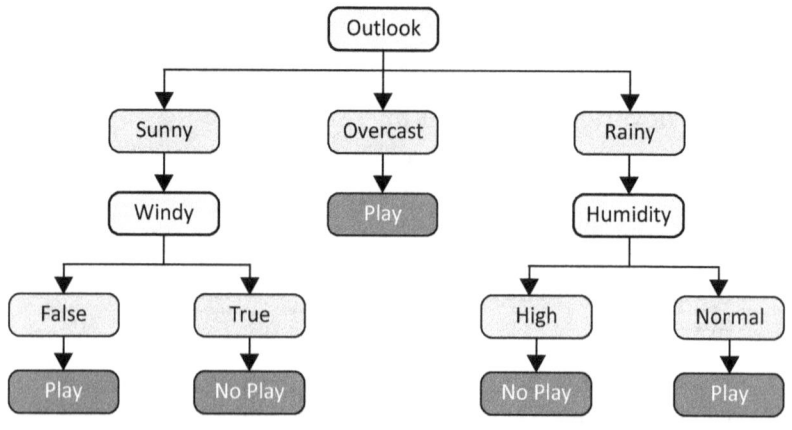

Support Vector Machines (SVM)

Generally, support vector machines (SVMs) are viewed as a classification algorithm, but they can be utilized for both classification and regression problems. It can effortlessly manage several continuous and categorical variables. SVMs function by identifying the best hyperplane that most effectively separates different classes in the feature space. To tackle non-linear classification issues, SVMs use kernel functions. In simple terms, kernel functions help SVMs find boundaries between classes even when the data isn't linearly separable in its original feature space. SVMs are best suited for high-dimensional data, where the number of features is large compared to the number of data points. However, SVMs may be costly in terms of computation and harder to interpret when compared to other algorithms.

Key Concepts

- **Hyperplane:** A decision boundary in a space that is high-dimensional that separates different classes.

- **Support vectors:** The data points closest to the decision boundary. These are critical in defining the hyperplane.

- **Margin:** The distance between the hyperplane and the support vectors. SVM tries to maximize this. A margin boundary is a hyperplane that maximizes the margin between two classes.

- **Kernel trick:** When the data is not linearly separable, SVM uses kernel functions to project the data into a higher-dimensional space where a linear separator can be found.

Mathematical understanding of SVM: Let's consider a problem with binary classification, which has two classes, labeled as +1 and –1. We have a training dataset consisting of input feature vectors (X) and their corresponding class labels (Y).

The equation for the linear hyperplane can be written as: $wTx+b=0$, where w is the normal vector to the hyperplane (the direction perpendicular to it). b is the offset or bias term, representing the distance of the hyperplane from the origin along the normal vector w.

EXAMPLE

Real-World Use Case: SVM for Tumor Classification

Doctors often need to decide whether a tumor is benign (non-cancerous) or malignant (cancerous). Luckily, we have historical data from many patients, and it includes features like the size, shape, and texture of their cells as measured in medical tests.

SVM is a machine learning method that performs exceptionally well when we aim to categorize items into two categories, such as in this instance: benign versus malignant tumors. We provide the algorithm with information from earlier patients. Every patient possesses a collection of features. The SVM analyzes this information and understands how to create a boundary (either a line or a curve) that distinguishes benign instances from malignant ones.

It accomplishes this by determining the optimal margin between the two classes, indicating the boundary is maximally distant from both sets of data. After training, when we present the model with a new patient's information, it applies the boundary it has learned to determine whether the tumor is probably benign or malignant.

K-Nearest Neighbors (KNN)

K-nearest neighbors (KNN) may be the most straightforward machine learning algorithm available.

It does not assume anything regarding the underlying data distribution as it relies solely on proximity. KNN is a simple instance-driven learning method that categorizes a new data point according to the majority vote of its "k" nearest neighbors within the feature space. It doesn't involve a traditional training phase, but it stores the data and performs all computations during the prediction, which makes it a bit sluggish.

Figure 3.8 | **Visual representation of k-nearest neighbors**

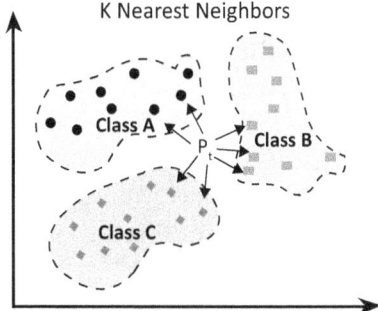

Imagine, on a Friday night, you are trying to pick a movie. You reach out to 5 of your closest friends (k = 5) for recommendations. If 3 of them suggest the same movie, then you proceed with that one. That's how KNN works, it makes predictions based on majority votes among the closest data points.

How KNN actually works:

1. Choose a value for **k** (the number of neighbors).
2. For a new data point, compute the **distance** to all other points in the dataset.
3. Select the **k-nearest neighbors**.
4. Assign the class based on the majority label among those neighbors.

KNN largely depends on the type of distance metric you choose. **Euclidean distance** is the most common distance measurement used to find the distance between two points in space. Think of it as a ruler used to measure the distance between two points.

For example, to find the distance between two points A and B with coordinates $A = (x_1, y_1)$ and $B = (x_2, y_2)$, we use the following formula:

$$\text{Distance} = \sqrt{\left(x_2 - x_1\right)^2 + \left(y_2 - y_1\right)^2}$$

3.2.1 Performance Metrics for Classification

Once a classification model is built, it's important to evaluate how well it performs. As briefly covered in Chapter 2, this is done using various performance metrics, which help us understand the strengths and limitations of the model beyond simply making predictions.

Below are some commonly used metrics for evaluating classification models:

1. **Accuracy:** It is the proportion of correctly classified instances out of the total predictions. It measures the overall correctness of the model. It is useful when the classes are balanced.

$$\text{Accuracy} = \frac{TP + TN}{TP + TN + FP + FN}$$

TP = True Positive

TN = True Negative

FP = False Positive

FN = False Negative

2. **Precision:** It is the ratio of true positive predictions to the total predicted positives. It measures how many of the predicted positive cases were actually positive, showcasing the model's exactness. It becomes very critical when false positives are costly (e.g., spam detection, fraud alerts).

$$\text{Precision} = \frac{TP}{TP + FP}$$

3. **Recall (Sensitivity):** It refers to the ratio of true positive predictions to all actual positives. It measures how many actual positive cases the model correctly identified. It becomes crucial when false negatives are costly (e.g., diagnosing diseases).

$$\text{Recall} = \frac{TP}{TP + FN}$$

4. **F1 Score:** It is the harmonic mean of precision and recall, which takes into consideration both measures in one score. It is especially useful when you have uneven class distribution and you want a balance between precision and recall.

$$\text{F1 Score} = 2 \times \frac{\text{Precision} \times \text{Recall}}{\text{Precision} + \text{Recall}}$$

5. **Confusion Matrix:** It is a detailed table that breaks down the performance by showing true positives, true negatives, false positives, and false negatives. It gives a complete picture of how the classification model is performing.

6. **ROC-AUC:** It is the area under the "receiver operating characteristic" curve, which helps us understand the model's ability to distinguish between classes.

Figure 3.9 A graphical representation of ROC and AUC

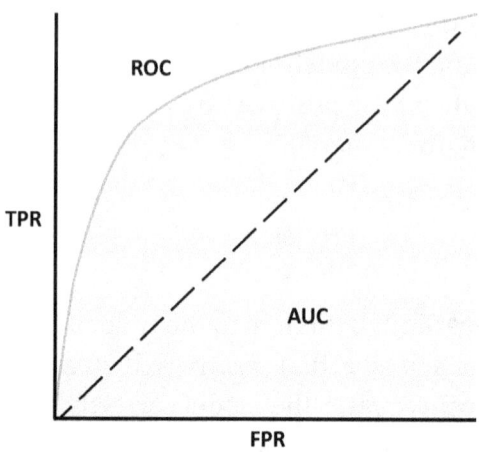

ROC curve: A plot that shows the trade-off between True Positive Rate (Recall) and False Positive Rate (FPR = FP / (FP + TN)) at various threshold settings.

AUC (Area Under the Curve): A single-value metric that summarizes the model's ability to distinguish between classes.

- **AUC = 1.0:** Perfect model
- **AUC = 0.5:** No better than random guessing

3.3 Clustering

Clustering is an unsupervised machine learning technique used to group data points into clusters based on their similarities. It does not use any training dataset, and there are no predefined labels. It allows the algorithm to identify inherent groupings within the data. In contrast to classification, clustering operates without labels as it identifies patterns on its own. This makes it especially useful for segmenting markets and identifying anomalies.

Clustering uses statistical concepts to split a dataset into subsets with similar features, grouping objects to establish relationships among them.

Figure 3.10 Data before and after clustering

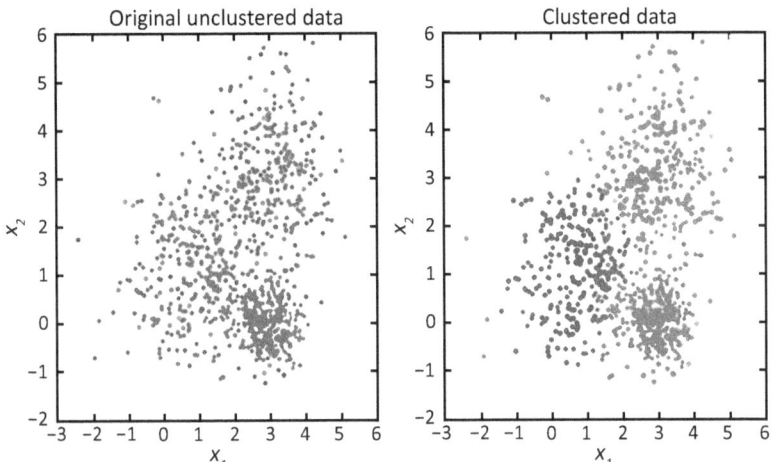

3.3.1 K-means Clustering

K-means is one of the most fundamental unsupervised learning algorithms used for clustering. However, selecting the appropriate number of clusters (k) requires careful consideration. It follows a simple procedure of classifying a given dataset into a number of clusters, defined by the letter "k", which is fixed beforehand. K-means identifies the k centroids (or centers) of these clusters. The "means" in K-means refers to calculating the average of the data points when finding these centroids.

In K-means clustering, there are two main methods for finding the optimal value of k: the Elbow method and the Silhouette method.

The Elbow method works by running the algorithm multiple times, with an increasing number of clusters. A clustering score, such as the within-cluster sum of squares (WCSS), is calculated each time and then plotted against the number of clusters. The goal is to identify the "elbow point" where the rate of decrease in WCSS sharply slows down, indicating a suitable value for k. However, the Elbow method may sometimes produce ambiguous results, making it difficult to identify the optimal number of clusters.

Figure 3.11 **Elbow method in K-means clustering**

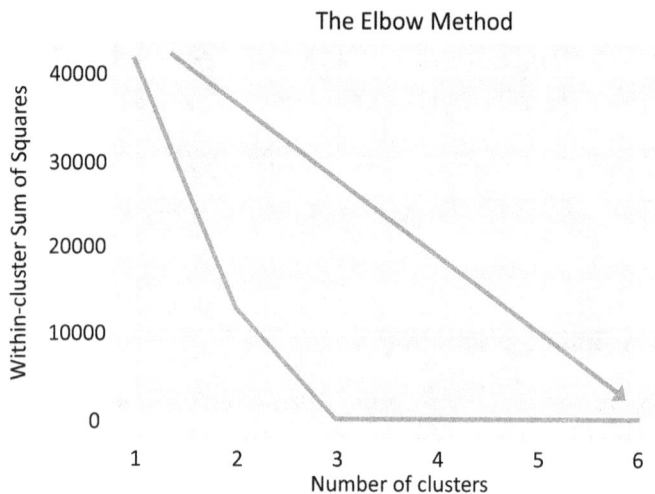

The silhouette method measures how similar a point is to its own cluster compared to other clusters. The range of the silhouette value is between +1 to –1. A high value is desirable and indicates that the point is placed in the correct cluster. A negative silhouette value suggests that the point may have been assigned to the wrong cluster, possibly due to having too many or too few clusters.

Figure 3.12 Silhouette method for cluster evaluation

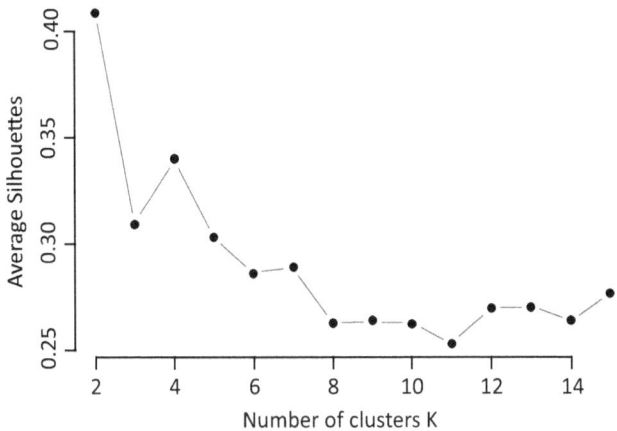

3.3.2 Hierarchical Clustering

Hierarchical clustering presents a different approach by forming a tree-like arrangement of clusters. This can be especially beneficial when you're uncertain about how many groups exist in your data. density-based spatial clustering of applications with noise (DBSCAN) is highly effective in identifying clusters of various shapes and detecting outliers, making it essential for anomaly detection systems.

Hierarchical clustering is an algorithm that groups similar objects into clusters. The result is a set of clusters, where each cluster is distinct from every other cluster, and the objects within each cluster are similar to each other. The algorithm builds a hierarchy of clusters, starting with each data point assigned to its own cluster. Then, the two nearest clusters are merged into the same cluster. It terminates when only a single cluster is left.

This algorithm can be implemented using both bottom up (agglomerative) and top down (divisive) approaches. The decision to merge two clusters is based on distance metrics that determine the closeness of clusters. Common distance metrics include:

- Euclidean distance
- Manhattan distance
- Maximum distance
- Mahalanobis distance

Figure 3.13 How agglomerative and divisive clustering build clusters differently

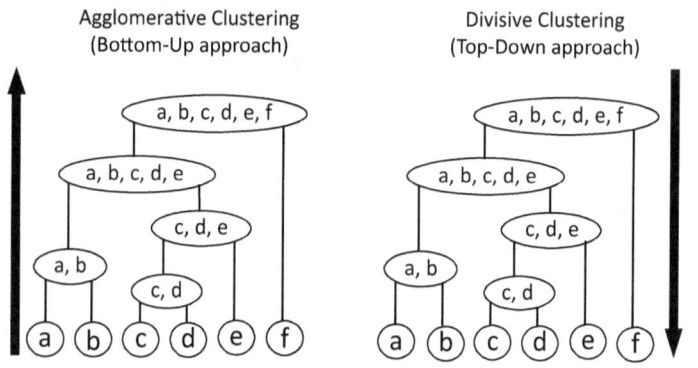

3.4 Key ML Algorithms and When to Use Them

In the world of ML algorithms, choosing the right algorithm depends on the type of problem you are trying to solve. It could involve predicting values or classifying outcomes. Here is a list of widely used ML algorithms, including their categories, ideal use cases, and examples that demonstrate when and why each is used.

Linear Regression

Category: Supervised (regression)

When to utilize:

- When the target variable is numerical, for example, forecasting property values or sales income

- When there is a straight correlation between dependent and independent variables

Use-cases:
- Predicting sales using past data
- Assessing the effect of marketing expenditure on income

Logistic Regression

Category: Supervised (categorization)
When to utilize:
- For tasks involving binary classification, such as yes/no or 0/1 results
- When the target variable is categorical, and there is a need for probabilities

Use-cases:
- Anticipating customer turnover
- Classifying email spam

Tree-based Models

Category: Supervised (classification and regression)
When to utilize:
- When understanding is crucial, for instance, recognizing decision-making procedures
- For datasets exhibiting non-linear connections between attributes and results

Use-cases:
- Processing approval for loans in banking institutions
- Categorizing patients according to their medical symptoms

Random Forest

Category: Supervised (classification and regression)
When to utilize:
- When you require great precision and interpretability is less important

- For managing extensive datasets characterized by high dimensionality and missing data

Use-cases:
- Forecasting stock market movements
- Identifying illnesses through various symptoms

K-Nearest Neighbors (KNN)

Category: Supervised (classification and prediction)

When to utilize:
- When you require a straightforward, non-parametric method
- For small datasets where processing time is not an issue

Use-cases:
- Suggesting films according to individual tastes
- Identifying fraudulent activities

3.5 Application of Machine Learning Algorithms

Machine learning has evolved over the past decade from being just a buzzword. Today, it's a powerful technology transforming industries and lives across the globe. From enhancing Netflix recommendations to facilitating early disease detection, ML algorithms are driving innovation and efficiency. Let's take a look at several key uses of ML across industries and see how these algorithms are producing real impact.

Retail

Retailers encounter intense rivalry and must provide personalized experiences to keep customers engaged. Recommendation systems using collaborative filtering and matrix factorization propose items according to previous purchases and browsing behavior. K-means clustering assists in dividing customers into high-value and budget-friendly categories for focused marketing efforts. For example, an online shopping site utilizes machine learning to forecast which customers may leave and provides incentives to retain them.

Healthcare

Correct and timely disease diagnosis can be life-saving. Conventional approaches frequently depend on personal interpretation and restricted data. However, classification techniques such as logistic regression and decision trees are built to forecast diseases like diabetes or cancer using patient information. Neural networks drive sophisticated medical imaging technologies. They aid in identifying irregularities in an X-ray or a magnetic resonance imaging (MRI). For example, hospitals use ML algorithms to examine patient data and forecast diseases to facilitate proactive treatment.

Finance

Fraudulent activities lead to billions of dollars of losses each year. This makes risk management a crucial focus for financial organizations. Anomaly detection techniques, such as clustering, uncover unusual patterns within transactional data. For instance, a credit card firm employs real-time machine learning models to identify unusual transactions. This helps prevent fraud before it happens.

Manufacturing

Anticipating equipment malfunctions and enhancing production efficiency are essential for minimizing downtime and expenses. Predictive maintenance algorithms assess sensor information from equipment to anticipate failures. Clustering algorithms categorize similar production flaws to enhance quality assurance. For example, a car manufacturer deploys ML algorithms to predict demand for various car models and modify production plans accordingly.

Education

Uniform education systems do not address individual learning requirements. NLP and Generative AI (GenAI) techniques fill these gaps by evaluating student performance as well as creating course content. Clustering organizes students with comparable learning styles to provide customized resources.

Many educational technology platforms employ machine learning to forecast which learners may require additional assistance by analyzing their engagement metrics. Virtual tutors, driven by GenAI, offer tailored teaching and immediate responses. This helps in increasing the availability of virtual tutors 24/7.

In conclusion, machine learning algorithms have proven to be highly effective in a wide range of applications, from enhancing educational tools to personalizing user experiences. These techniques enable systems to learn from data, make predictions, and adapt over time, improving both efficiency and outcomes. As we transition to the next chapter, we will explore deep learning, a more advanced subset of machine learning, which leverages complex neural networks to solve even more intricate problems and push the boundaries of AI capabilities.

Chapter Summary

- The real strength of machine learning is in its adaptability, and the three key types of ML algorithms are regression, classification and clustering.

- Regression is used to predict continuous outcomes (e.g., sales prediction, house prices). Classification groups data into categories (e.g., spam detection, loan approval).

- This chapter also highlights popular algorithms like clustering, decision trees, SVM, and KNN.

- Whether it's a hospital saving lives via early detection, a retailer satisfying customers with tailored interactions, or a logistics company streamlining processes, ML algorithms are the catalyst for impactful transformation.

- As a data scientist, it's crucial to not only understand these algorithms but also to implement them carefully.

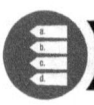 **Quiz**

1. **Which machine learning technique is primarily used to predict continuous outcomes?**

    a. Classification
    b. Regression
    c. Clustering
    d. Reinforcement learning

2. **Which of the following is an example of a regression algorithm?**

    a. Logistic regression
    b. Linear regression
    c. Decision trees
    d. Naive Bayes

3. **In linear regression, what does the assumption of "linearity" refer to?**

    a. The predictors and target have a straight-line relationship.
    b. The errors are normally distributed.
    c. The predictors are independent of each other.
    d. The residuals have equal variance.

4. **Which performance metric in regression measures the average squared difference between predicted and actual values?**

    a. Mean absolute error (MAE)
    b. R-squared
    c. Mean squared error (MSE)
    d. Adjusted R-squared

5. **What is the primary goal of classification algorithms?**
   a. Predicting continuous numerical values
   b. Grouping data into clusters
   c. Categorizing data into predefined groups
   d. Reducing the number of features

6. **Which metric is most suitable for evaluating a classification model's balance between precision and recall?**
   a. Accuracy
   b. F1 score
   c. R-squared
   d. Mean absolute error

7. **Logistic regression is best used for which type of problem?**
   a. Multi-class classification with more than two outcomes
   b. Regression predicting continuous values
   c. Binary classification tasks
   d. Unsupervised clustering

8. **A practical application of machine learning in retail is:**
   a. Predicting property prices using linear regression
   b. Classifying emails as spam or not spam
   c. Using Random Forest to predict customer churn
   d. Detecting spelling errors

9. Which metric is commonly used to evaluate the quality of clusters in unsupervised learning?
   a. Silhouette score
   b. F1 score
   c. R-squared
   d. Mean Squared Error

10. Which clustering algorithm is particularly effective for detecting clusters of arbitrary shape and handling noise?
    a. K-means
    b. Hierarchical clustering
    c. DBSCAN
    d. Gaussian mixture models

Answers

1 – b	2 – b	3 – a	4 – c	5 – c
6 – b	7 – c	8 – c	9 – a	10 – c

CHAPTER 4

Deep Learning

Key Learning Objectives

- Learn the fundamentals of deep learning and neural networks.
- Understand the architecture and workings of CNN and RNN.
- Explore how deep learning algorithms gained popularity.
- Discover practical business applications of deep learning algorithms.

In this chapter, we will explore the core principles of deep learning and examine how its algorithms are applied across different industries to solve real-world problems.

4.1 Introduction to Deep Learning (DL)

Deep learning is a more advanced domain within the AI and ML field that mimics the structure of the human brain to analyze data. Deep learning algorithms attempt to draw conclusions in a way similar to humans, by continuously analyzing data using a logical structure called a neural network. We were briefly introduced to neural networks in Chapter 2, where we saw how the depth of these networks contributes to the power and effectiveness of deep learning. In this chapter, we will dive deeper into the functioning of neural networks.

At the core of any neural network is the neuron, which is also known as the perceptron. It is the building block of a neural network. While ML algorithms mostly do their work using statistical techniques, DL relies on a logical structure inspired by the human brain. The layers of neurons in these networks process information step by step. While it mimics the brain's functioning, the learning process is deeply embedded in mathematical techniques, which helps neural networks learn patterns from data efficiently.

Deep learning models are famous for their capacity to understand intricate patterns, yet they impose considerable practical requirements. A key issue is their reliance on data—these models need large quantities of labeled data to train successfully. Lacking adequate data, the models might find it difficult to generalize, resulting in poor performance.

Moreover, the intricacy and depth of these networks imply that training durations can be lengthy, frequently necessitating iterative methods over substantial datasets. A major benefit, however, is the automatic extraction of features, which lessens the reliance on manual feature selection.

Due to their computational intensity, deep learning models typically require specialized hardware such as graphics processing units (GPUs) or tensor processing units (TPUs), which are optimized for the matrix operations that underpin neural network training.

4.1.1 Evolution of Deep Learning

Neural networks have continuously evolved over the last 75 years. In this section, we'll take a closer look at how they have developed and improved over time.

The perceptron was introduced during the 1950s, as an early model of a neural network that could solve basic logic problems like AND and OR. It sparked excitement as a possible start to AI's golden age. The hype faded a bit during the 1970s, when it was discovered that perceptrons couldn't solve XOR problems, which is a type of logic that requires more complex thinking. This led to disillusionment and what's referred to as AI's first "winter."

Geoffrey Hinton introduced multilayer perceptrons (MLPs) with hidden layers and non-linear activation functions like sigmoid, enabling networks to learn complex patterns (including XOR). This marked the real beginning of deep learning in the 1980s. However, during the 1990s, neural networks stalled due to limited computational power and the focus shifted to simpler algorithms like Support Vector Machines (SVMs).

Geoffrey Hinton returned in the 2000s with deep learning and multiple hidden layers. Computational advancements made the concept more viable, though not mainstream.

In the 2010s, with the rise of GPUs and cloud computing, deep learning became widely accessible and began outperforming traditional ML methods in vision, speech, and language tasks. Today, deep learning drives breakthroughs in GenAI, NLP, and computer vision. Geoffrey Hinton, hailed as the godfather of modern AI, continues to push boundaries with innovations.

Figure 4.1　Brief history of neural networks

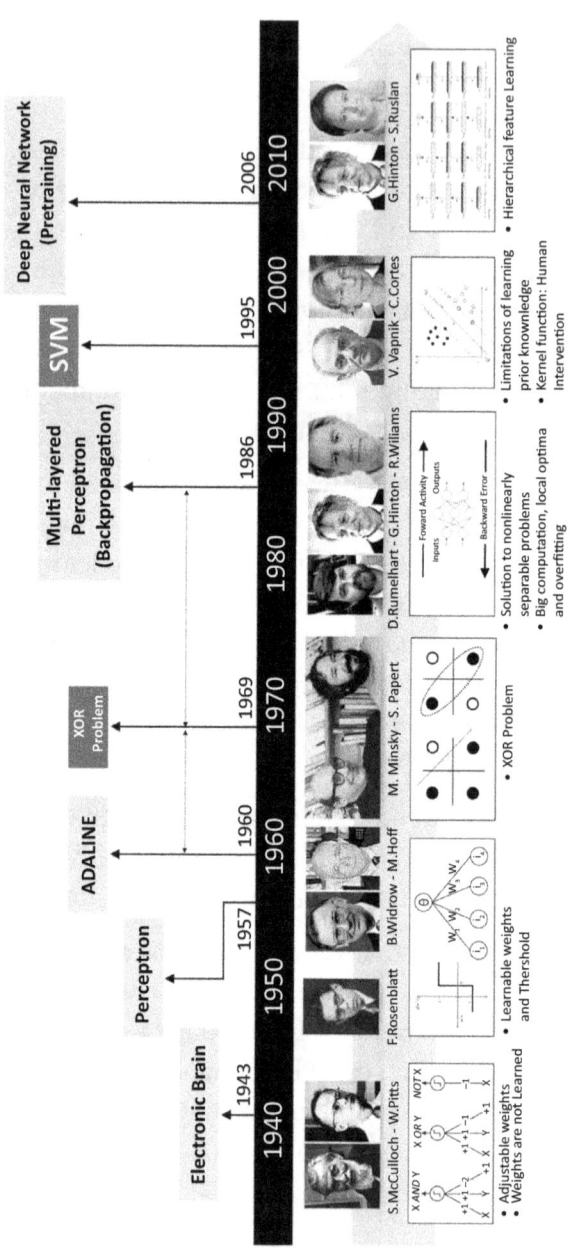

Source: Serengil, S. I. (2017). Evolution of neural networks. Sefiks. https://sefiks. com/2017/10/14/evolution-of-neural-networks/

Building effective deep learning systems is not just about building models, but it requires thoughtful consideration of several key factors. Let's try to understand some of them.

4.1.2 Primary Considerations While Designing Deep Learning-Based Solutions

Data Dependency

Deep learning requires significantly more data compared to machine learning. Therefore, if you are working on a problem, you can apply deep learning only when you have a large amount of data. With access to more data, the performance of DL becomes more reliable.

Training Time

Again, DL models are too complex, which is why their training time is significantly higher compared to ML. Prediction time in deep learning is generally higher in DL due to the complexity of its models. However, in comparison to some ML algorithms, like k-nearest neighbors, deep learning models can also have a slower prediction time. So, the prediction time can vary depending on the specific algorithm being used.

Feature Selection

DL automatically extracts relevant features, which is referred to as representation learning. In contrast with traditional machine learning, you need to manually extract and define the important features. For example, in resume-based selection, a deep learning model can directly learn important features from the resume itself, whereas in machine learning, you would first need to manually define which features are important.

Hardware Requirements

ML models can be trained on a central processing unit (CPU), but deep learning requires GPUs for efficient computation due to its complex matrix operations. Training deep learning models on a CPU would be significantly slower.

Risk of Overfitting

Due to their high capacity and flexibility, deep learning models are particularly prone to overfitting. To prevent this, researchers use techniques like dropout (randomly turning off parts of the model during training), early stopping (stopping training before the model starts overfitting), and data augmentation (slightly changing the training data to make it more diverse). These techniques help the model learn better and work well on new data.

4.2 Neural Networks

Neural networks are inspired by the structure of the human brain, where artificial "neurons" are interconnected and work together to recognize patterns and solve complex problems. Just as neurons process signals in the brain, neural networks process information in layers of interconnected nodes. They are basically machine learning systems modeled after the human brain, consisting of interconnected layers of synthetic neurons.

Figure 4.2   How signal communication occurs through neurons in human brain

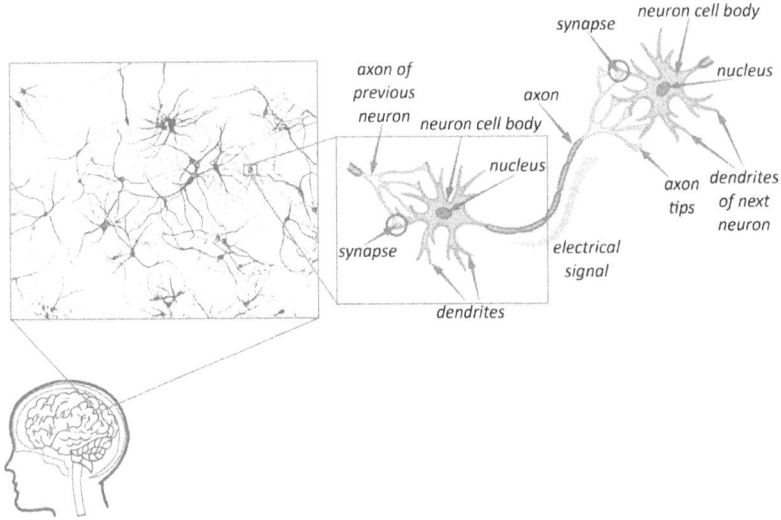

Source: Jayakumar, P. (2021). The McCulloch-Pitts ANN: "Calculus based biological computational model that made the base of today's deep learning". CodeX (Medium). https://medium.com/codex/the-mcculloch-pitts-ann-ba8c887769fc

In the human brain, a typical neuron collects signals from others through a host of fine structures called dendrites. The neuron sends out spikes of electrical activity through a long, thin strand known as an axon, which splits into thousands of branches. At the end of each branch, a structure called a synapse converts the activity from the axon into electrical effects that inhibit or excite activity in the connected neurons.

Similarly, neural networks learn to recognize complex patterns by adjusting the weights of the connections between neurons during training. As data flows through the network, each neuron applies a mathematical transformation using weights and biases. An activation function is then applied to introduce non-linearity, allowing the network to model complex relationships in the data.

The forward propagation process calculates the network's output, whereas backpropagation (which we will understand in detail in section 4.2.2) modifies the weights by sending error signals backward, progressively enhancing accuracy. This adaptability makes them perfect for activities like image recognition, natural language processing, and others.

Let's explore the fundamental components of neural networks to better understand how they work.

Figure 4.3   What a neural network looks like

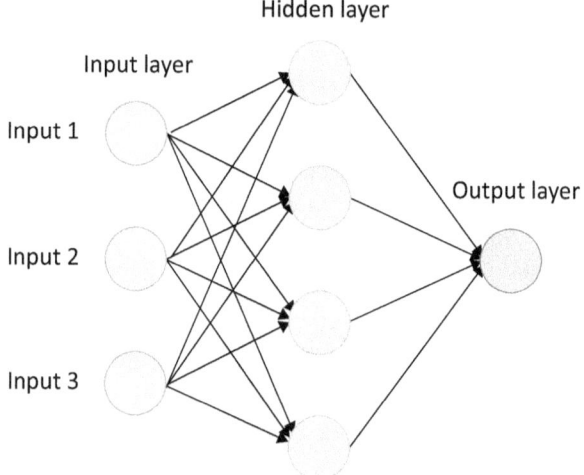

4.2.1 Components of Neural Networks

Neural networks consist of multiple essential and interconnected elements that collaboratively handle data, recognize patterns, and generate predictions. Grasping these elements is crucial for comprehending how deep learning models operate. Let's understand each of these fundamental components in detail.

Weights and Biases

Both these elements are crucial parameters. Weights control the connection strength between neurons, while biases shift the activation function to adjust outputs independently of inputs. Together, they help the network learn and improve accuracy. Weights are adjustable parameters that define the intensity and orientation of the link between two neurons. A greater weight indicates a more significant impact of the input on the neuron's output. Biases are extra parameters that permit the activation function to shift, helping the model better align with the data. Throughout training, optimization algorithms, such as gradient descent, adjust both weights and biases to reduce the loss function and enhance model accuracy.

Activation Functions

Activation functions play an important role in how a neural network learns. They help the network understand and learn complex patterns in the data by adding something called non-linearity. Without them, the network would only be able to learn simple, straight-line relationships.

After each neuron (or node) in the network calculates a value (called a weighted sum), the activation function decides what the output of that neuron should be. This output is usually limited to a certain range.

Here are some common activation functions:

- **ReLU (Rectified Linear Unit):** This is the most popular one. It gives a 0 if the input is negative, and just passes the input through if it's positive. It's simple and helps prevent some common training problems, like the vanishing gradient (when learning slows down too much).

- **Sigmoid:** This function squashes values between 0 and 1, making it useful for problems where the output is a yes/no (binary) answer.

- **Tanh:** Similar to sigmoid, it gives outputs between −1 and 1. It's often used in certain types of networks like RNNs, which are designed to handle sequential data like text.

- **Softmax:** This function is used when the network needs to choose between multiple categories. It turns numbers into probabilities that all add up to 1.

Point to Remember

The choice of activation function can affect how fast the network learns and how well it performs.

Input Layer

It refers to the first layer of nodes and is the starting point of any neural network. It's where the network receives raw data—like numbers, images, or text. There are no weights in the input layer because this layer receives input data from outside. Each node in this layer represents a feature or variable from the input dataset. It does not perform any computation, but simply passes the raw data into the network. For example, if you're working with an image of size 28×28 pixels, the input layer will have 784 nodes (28×28). This layer is crucial and helps the network understand how much information it is receiving from the beginning.

Output Layer

The output layer is the last layer in the network and is tasked with generating the prediction. It gives the final result and uses the weights from the hidden layer. The structure varies based on the task type, such as a single neuron utilizing a sigmoid activation for binary classification or several neurons employing a softmax activation for multi-class classification. The final results are obtained by utilizing what the network has learned in earlier steps and applying a mathematical rule to decide the final output.

Hidden Layer

Hidden layers exist between the input and the output. They carry out the majority of the significant work by acquiring hierarchical representations of data. It processes input data and can have multiple layers within. It uses weights to combine inputs and biases to shift the output. The hidden layer applies an activation function to produce the final output. Every neuron in a hidden layer calculates a weighted sum of its inputs, includes a bias term, and uses an activation function (such as ReLU, tanh, or sigmoid). The depth (count of hidden layers) and width (count of neurons per layer) greatly influence the capacity of the network to learn intricate features, particularly in deep neural networks.

4.2.2 Forward and Backward Propagation

In forward propagation, the flow of data through the neural network occurs layer by layer, starting from the input layer. Within this, each layer processes the data by applying a weighted sum of the inputs, adding a bias term, and passing the result through an activation function. This process continues until the output layer produces the final prediction or result.

| **Figure 4.4** | **Forward and backward propagation in a neural network** |

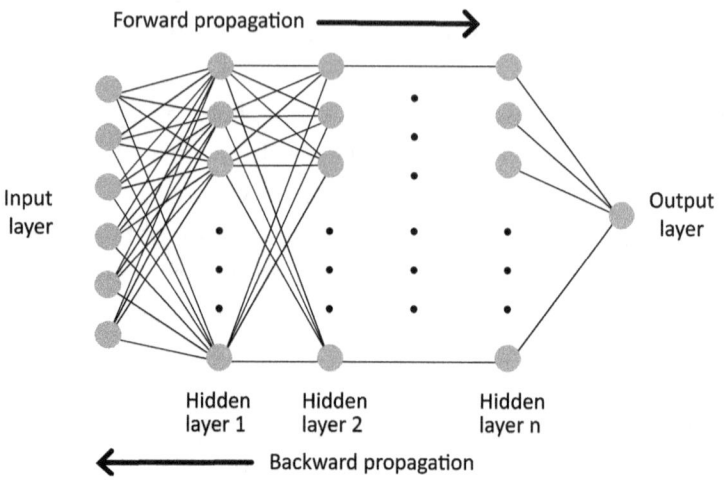

In backpropagation, you train the neural network by updating the weights on the backward pass, which helps improve the model's performance. It is an essential algorithm that enables a neural network to learn from its errors. It operates by modifying the network's weights so that the error is reduced between the predicted output and the actual output. The procedure occurs in two primary stages:

1. **Forward Pass:** The input goes through the network to make a prediction.

2. **Backward Pass (Backpropagation):** The error is computed, and subsequently, the model traverses backward to adjust the weights using calculus (specifically, the chain rule for derivatives).

Now, imagine the neural network produced a wrong prediction. The loss function measures the degree of error in the prediction. To correct this error, the network needs to understand how each weight contributed to it. This is where gradients come in. A gradient is a partial derivative that tells us how much a small change in a particular weight will affect the loss. By computing these gradients, the network learns which weights to adjust, and by how much, to reduce future errors.

This entire process of measuring the error, calculating gradients, and updating the weights is known as backpropagation. It's the backbone of learning in neural networks.

Methods for weight adjustment: After computing the gradients, we adjust the weights by utilizing optimization algorithms such as:

- Gradient Descent (GD): Adjusts weights toward the direction of the negative gradient.

- Stochastic Gradient Descent (SGD): Adjusts weights for every training instance, incorporating randomness, which can help the model learn faster and avoid getting stuck in the wrong place.

- Adam (Adaptive Moment Estimation): A more advanced optimizer that combines ideas from Momentum (which helps smooth out updates) and RMSProp (which adapts learning rates); adjusts the learning rate for every weight separately.

Sample pseudocode for backpropagation: Here's a simplified pseudocode outline showing the key steps involved in forward and backward passes:

```
# Forward Pass
  for each layer in network:
    z = weight * input + bias
    activation = activation_function(z)
# Compute Loss
  loss = loss_function(predicted_output, actual_output)
# Backward Pass
  for each layer in reverse:
```

```
        dLoss/dActivation = derivative_of_loss_function()
        dActivation/dZ = derivative_of_activation_function()
        dLoss/dWeight = dLoss/dActivation * dActivation/dZ *
    input
        weight = weight - learning_rate * dLoss/dWeight
```

Having explored how neural networks adjust their weights using optimization algorithms, we can now consider how these methods are applied in more complex network architectures, such as convolutional or recurrent neural networks.

4.2.3 Deep Neural Networks (DNN)

A deep neural network is a multi-layered neural network. Usually there are many hidden layers in a deep neural network. There is no consensus on the number of hidden layers to call it a "deep" net; however, more than two hidden layers can sometimes be considered "deep." Due to the presence of many layers and the associated non-linear operations, the input is transformed at the output through complex non-linear changes. This helps deep neural networks to model very complex non-linear decision boundaries for pattern classification tasks.

Moreover, such networks have the ability to automatically extract features from the given input with little or no need for manual feature engineering. Therefore, raw data (e.g., images, audio signals, text, etc.) can be fed into such networks. These deep neural networks can represent the input as a hierarchy of important features in the earlier layers and subsequently use these features in the final layers to make suitable decisions (e.g., pattern classification, image recognition, object detection, text classification, etc.).

Figure 4.5 Sample DNN

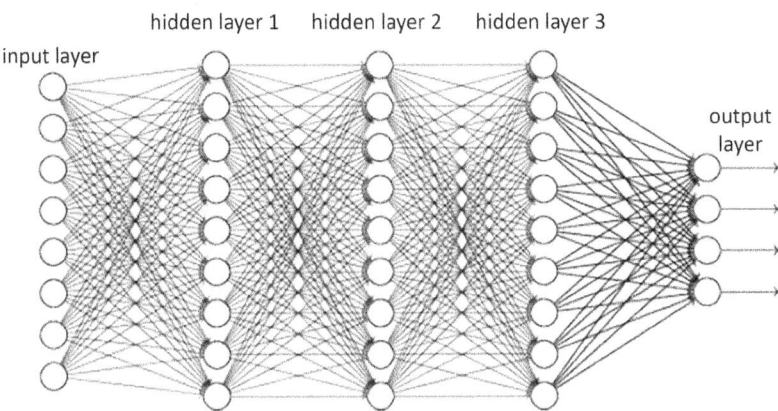

Source: Elsevier. (n.d.). Deep Neural Network – An Overview. In ScienceDirect.
https://www.sciencedirect.com/topics/engineering/deep-neural-network

Since we have already covered the input layer, hidden layer and the output later in the previous section, in this section we will cover the other layers like dropout and fully connected layers.

Figure 4.6 Sample fully connected layer and dropout layer

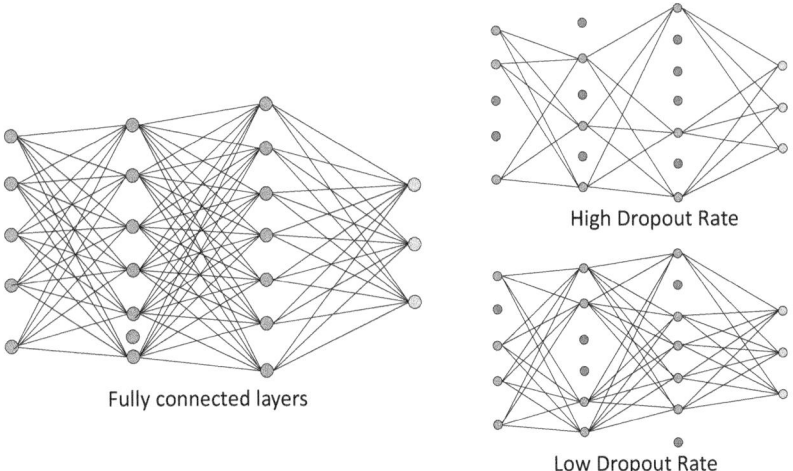

Fully connected layers

High Dropout Rate

Low Dropout Rate

Fully Connected Layer

A fully connected (FC) layer is a standard component of deep neural networks, particularly in architectures like convolutional neural networks (CNNs). This layer is typically placed toward the end of the network, where it transforms the learned, high-level features into a flattened one-dimensional vector used for final classification or regression.

In this layer, every neuron is connected to all neurons in the preceding layer, merging the spatially distributed information into a cohesive prediction. Fundamentally, it functions as a conventional neural network layer, where the acquired features are used to produce the final output. The fully connected layer plays an essential role in understanding the high-level representations created by previous layers and converting them into actionable outcomes.

Dropout

Dropout is a regularization method employed to avoid overfitting in neural networks by randomly switching off a portion of neurons during training. This procedure compels the network to acquire redundant representations and stops it from depending too much on any one neuron. Usually, a dropout rate, for example, 20% to 50%, is established to ascertain the fraction of neurons to exclude. This randomness helps the model become more resilient and improves its ability to generalize to new data.

It's important to note that dropout is only applied during training. During inference (when the model is making predictions), dropout is turned off, enabling the entire network to generate predictions using properly scaled weights.

4.3 Convolutional Neural Networks (CNNs)

CNNs are a class of neural networks that are primarily designed for handling image-based data. The name "convolutional" comes from a mathematical model called convolution. It is a mathematical operation that combines two functions to produce a third function expressing how the shape of one is modified by the other. At a high level, CNN identifies an image and assigns an appropriate label, as shown in Figure 4.7.

Figure 4.7 Example of CNN identifying an image

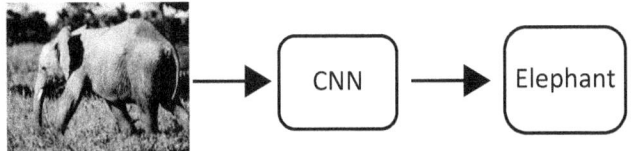

When compared to conventional neural networks, CNNs add filters to identify various patterns like edges, textures, and shapes. This makes them extremely proficient in computer vision-related tasks. They have become a very important algorithm within deep learning, particularly for tasks related to image and video analysis.

The CNN architecture has several types of layers: input layer, convolutional layer, pooling layer, and fully connected layer. Pooling layers in CNNs enhance the feature extraction by reducing spatial dimensions, which helps in lowering computational costs while retaining the essential information that is required.

These features are then fed into completely connected layers that combine the learned representations to perform various tasks like classification or object detection. Lastly, the dropout layers in CNNs are frequently used to prevent overfitting by randomly disabling some neurons during the entire training process.

The real-world application ranges from facial recognition systems to medical image assessment. Over a period of time, CNNs have revolutionized computer vision and continue to promote progress in visual data analysis.

To understand how CNNs achieve such remarkable performance in visual tasks, it's essential to look at the key layers that make up their architecture. Each layer plays a distinct role in transforming input data into meaningful patterns and predictions.

4.3.1 Key Layers in CNNs

Convolutional neural networks are specifically created for handling data with a grid-like structure, such as images. Their architecture consists of specialized layers that capture spatial hierarchies of features, facilitating strong pattern recognition abilities.

Figure 4.8 Architecture of CNN

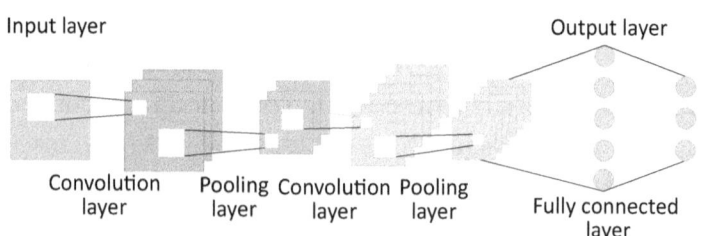

Source: Adapted from Gu, H., Wang, Y., Hong, S., & Gui, G. (2019). Blind channel identification aided generalized automatic modulation recognition based on deep learning. IEEE Access. https://doi.org/10.1109/ACCESS.2019.2934354.

Input layer: An image is the starting point in the architecture of a CNN. The input image can be an image of a human, animal, CCTV footage, or even medical scans like MRIs or CT scans. At a very simplistic level, all images can be represented by a matrix of numbers. Each number in the grid corresponds to a part of the image. Take a look at Figure 4.9, which shows a simple image of the letter T. We can turn this image into a matrix where the cells that contain parts of the letter T are given the value 0, and all the other cells are given the value 1.

Figure 4.9 **Image-to-matrix transformation for CNN processing**

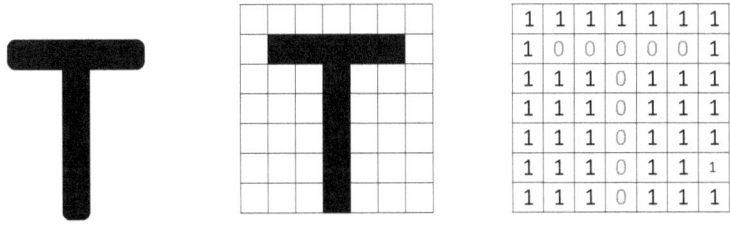

Convolutional layer: The convolutional layer applies filters to extract features from images. It is tasked with identifying local patterns in the input. A convolutional layer consists of two parts: (a) a filter, also known as feature detection, and (b) a feature map. Both the feature detector and the feature map are used to reshape and resize the input image to prepare it for further processing.

A feature detector (also called a filter or kernel) is a small grid of numbers, usually in an $n \times n$ shape. It moves across the image to look for specific patterns, such as edges or textures. As the filter slides over different parts of the image, it performs a simple math operation called a dot product. This helps create a new output called a feature map, which shows where certain patterns appear in the image. These feature maps are important because they help the next layers in the network learn more complex and detailed patterns. The operation is regulated by parameters such as:

- **Filter size** – how big the filter is
- **Stride** – how many steps the filter moves at a time
- **Padding** – whether extra space is added around the image, so the filter can cover the edges

These parameters affect how much detail is captured and how deep the understanding of the image becomes.

The filter "scans" the image and reduces its size while preserving the important components of that image as deemed important by the filter. So here, the input image is modified by a filter. This scanning happens by placing the filter (also called a feature detector) over small sections of the image, like laying a small grid on top of a larger one. The filter and the image overlap at corresponding cells (or elements of the matrix), and a calculation is performed at each step. The computation is done by multiplying the corresponding elements. This process is then repeated for all cells, which results in a new processed image: $(0\times0+0\times0+0\times1) + (0\times1+1\times0+0\times0) + (0\times0+0\times1+0\times1) = 0$. The visual representation in Figure 4.10 shows the filter's motion and the calculations carried out step by step.

Figure 4.10 Illustration of filter application in CNNs

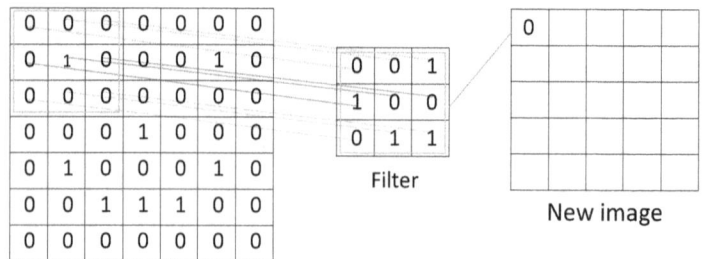

Input image

Filter

New image

When we place the filter at all possible positions of the input image, we get a reduced image, known as a feature map. In practice, we don't use just one filter; we use multiple filters, each designed to detect different patterns. As shown in Figure 4.11, using multiple filters means we create multiple feature maps, one for each filter. This results in several different versions of the same input image, with each feature map highlighting specific details. In this example, we are using 5 filters (feature detectors), which produce 5 corresponding feature maps.

Figure 4.11   Creating multiple feature maps using convolution filters

0	0	0	0	0	0	0
0	1	0	0	0	1	0
0	0	0	0	0	0	0
0	0	0	1	0	0	0
0	1	0	0	0	1	0
0	0	1	1	1	0	0
0	0	0	0	0	0	0

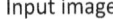 Input image    Multiple filters    Multiple features maps

Pooling layer: After processing our image through the convolutional layer, we have multiple feature maps of the image. The pooling layer takes this process further by just processing the subject of interest and ignoring other components of the image.

Let's say we are trying to recognize a cat in an image. Imagine the cat is sitting on a tree. By using the pooling layer, we can ignore all the tree related parts of the image and just process the cat. To identify whether the image has a cat in it or not, the neural network may look at the ears, eyes, whiskers and so on. So, the pooling layer identifies the important part of the image and extracts it while ignoring the rest. This is done again with the help of an $n \times n$ matrix.

For example, if we use a 2×2 kernel, we move it across the feature map and, for each 2×2 block, we pick the maximum number. This technique is called Max Pooling.

Take a look at Figure 4.12. The maximum number in each of the colored boxes from the feature map are selected in the pooled feature map. This helps retain only the strongest features, which are often the most essential for recognizing the object, while ignoring weaker or unnecessary details.

Figure 4.12 **Example of max pooling in CNNs**

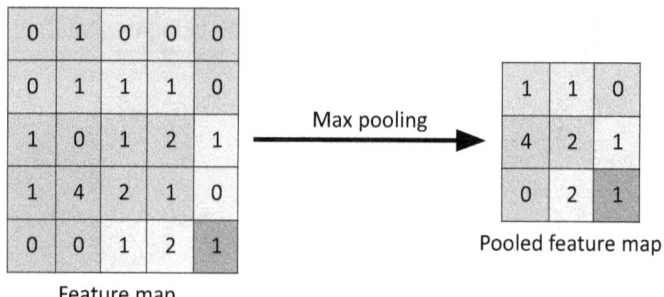

Feature map

Max pooling

Pooled feature map

Flattening: As the name suggests, flattening is the process of turning the pooled feature map into a single long column of numbers.

Let's say we have a 3×3 matrix after pooling. Flattening takes this matrix and converts it into a 9×1 column (since 3 × 3 = 9). In simple terms, it takes each row of the matrix and stacks them one below the other to form a single column. This step is important because it prepares the data to be fed into the fully connected layers of the neural network, where actual classification happens.

Take a look at Figure 4.13 where each row is represented with a different color. During flattening, all the rows are placed one on top of the other, forming a single vertical list of values.

Figure 4.13 Example of flattening process in CNN architecture

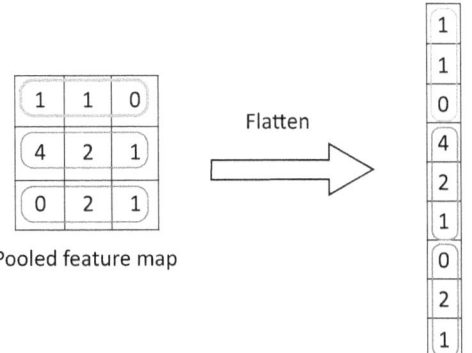

Pooled feature map

Flattened layer

Fully connected layer: This layer takes the flattened output from the previous layer and performs a matrix multiplication between the input values and a set of weights. After that, it adds a bias term and applies an activation function to introduce non-linearity.

In short, the fully connected layer combines all the features learned by the earlier layers to make the final decision. It is the last step in the CNN before the output is produced.

Figure 4.14 Fully connected layer for generating output predictions

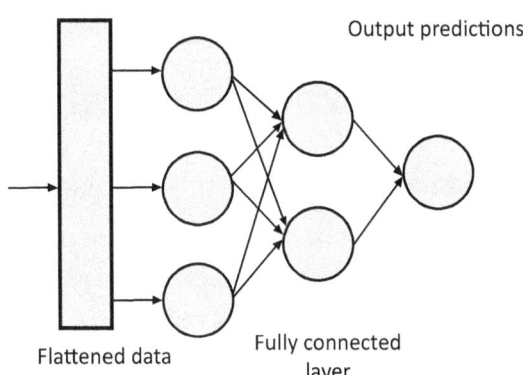

Output predictions

Flattened data

Fully connected layer

Convolutional neural networks (CNNs) have emerged as the foundation of contemporary computer vision. From basic image identification tasks to driving sophisticated applications in self-driving cars, facial recognition, and even healthcare diagnostics, CNNs have shown extraordinary versatility and precision.

Their architecture, which integrates convolutional layers, pooling layers, and fully connected layers, mimics how humans process visual information. Initially, CNNs concentrate on local patterns and then gradually understand more complex structures. By automatically learning features, reducing preprocessing, and scaling effectively, CNNs have transformed the way machines understand visual information.

As artificial intelligence continues to evolve, CNNs will keep progressing, facilitating real-time video analysis, medical image segmentation, augmented reality, and even generative uses. The future of AI is becoming increasingly visually intelligent, and CNNs are at the heart of this transformation.

4.4 Recurrent Neural Networks (RNNs)

Now that we are aware of how CNNs process image data, let's understand Recurrent Neural Networks (RNNs), which are focused on sequential data. RNNs have an internal memory that stores knowledge from previous stages and inputs, making them ideal for tasks where the order of information matters, such as time-series forecasting, speech recognition, and natural language processing.

RNN works on the principle of saving the output of a particular layer and feeding this back to the input. This is done to predict the output of the layer. Figure 4.15 illustrates how a feedforward neural network is converted into a recurrent neural network.

Figure 4.15 | RNN architecture

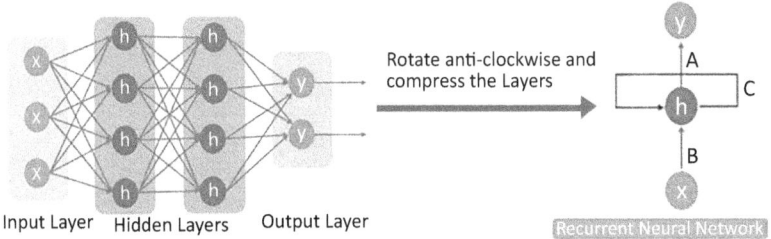

Source: Kalita, D. (2022). A brief overview of Recurrent Neural Networks (RNN). Analytics Vidhya. https://www.analyticsvidhya.com/blog/2022/03/a-brief-overview-of-recurrent-neural-networks-rnn/

The nodes in different layers of the neural network are compressed to form a single layer of recurrent neural networks.

Here, "x" is the input layer, "h" is the hidden layer, and "y" is the output layer. A, B, and C are the network parameters used to improve the output of the model. At any given time "t", the current input will be a combination of input at $x(t)$ and $x(t–1)$. The output at any given time is fed back to the network to enhance future predictions.

Traditional RNNs typically struggle with the vanishing gradient problem. This means they struggle to remember information from earlier in a sequence, which stops their ability to learn long-term dependencies. In order to fix this, advanced models such as Long Short-Term Memory (LSTM) networks and Gated Recurrent Units (GRUs) have been developed. These architectures incorporate special techniques to choose what information to retain or remove, thus, addressing the constraints of traditional RNNs.

In the upcoming section, we will understand the functions of RNNs and the variations, explaining how their memory components enable effective performance in fields like speech recognition, language modeling, and time-series forecasting.

4.4.1 Why RNN?

RNNs were created to address a few issues in the feedforward neural networks, which:

- Cannot handle sequential data
- Consider only the current input
- Cannot memorize previous inputs

RNNs can memorize previous inputs due to their internal memory. An RNN can handle sequential data, accepting the current input data and previously received inputs.

For example, in natural language processing, RNNs can be used to analyze the meaning of a sentence by considering the words that came before it. Similarly, in time-series analysis, RNNs can be used to predict the next value in a sequence by considering the previous values.

4.4.2 Types of RNNs

There are mainly three types of RNNs. Let's explore each one of them in detail:

Figure 4.16 **Difference between the three types of RNNs**

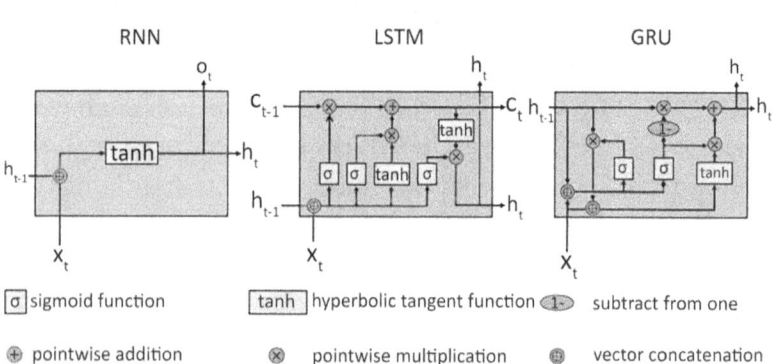

Source: Idrees, H. (2024). RNN vs. LSTM vs. GRU: A comprehensive guide to sequential data modeling. Medium. https://medium.com

Standard RNNs

Standard RNNs handle sequential data by using the output from earlier time steps as inputs for the present step.

This repetitive process enables them to grasp short-term relationships within sequences. However, as the length of the sequence grows, these networks frequently experience the vanishing gradient issue during backpropagation. This problem results in weaker gradient signals and, thus, complicates the model's ability to effectively learn long-term dependencies.

In RNNs, the sigmoid activation function maps input values to a range between 0 and 1. This is ideal for controlling how much information to retain or forget, especially in gated architectures like LSTMs and GRUs. It acts like an on/off switch for information flow.

Similarly, tanh (hyperbolic tangent) is an activation function that ranges between –1 and 1. It maintains zero-centered outputs, allowing the network to model both positive and negative relationships in the case of sequential data.

Long Short-Term Memory (LSTM)

LSTM addresses vanishing gradients through the use of memory cells and gating controls.

These networks use input, forget, and output gates to manage the information flow. It helps decide which data to keep or remove as necessary. This design enables LSTMs to efficiently recognize both short-term and long-term relationships in sequential information.

These gates use sigmoid activations to decide what information to retain, discard, or output, while a tanh layer scales the values flowing through the cell. This architecture allows LSTMs to maintain stable gradients during backpropagation through time (BPTT), enabling them to capture long-term dependencies more effectively than standard RNNs.

Gated Recurrent Units (GRUs)

GRUs provide a more streamlined option compared to LSTMs by merging the input and forget gates into one update gate. This simplified design minimizes the number of parameters and computational demands while effectively tackling the vanishing gradient problem. GRUs effectively capture time-based relationships in sequential data and frequently reach performance levels similar to LSTMs, rendering them a compelling choice for tasks where simplicity and speed are crucial.

This streamlined design leads to fewer parameters, making GRUs faster to train and less prone to overfitting on smaller datasets. Despite being simpler, GRUs retain temporal dependencies effectively and often achieve comparable or better performance than LSTMs, especially in real-time applications like chatbots, predictive text, and speech processing, where lower latency is essential.

4.4.3 Applications of RNNs

RNNs are designed to comprehend sequences, be it words, sound, or time-series information. This capability renders them highly valuable in various sectors. Let's explore some practical, real-life uses of RNNs in operation.

Speech recognition (e.g., Google Assistant, Siri): Whenever you ask Siri or Google Assistant a question, there's an RNN initiated behind the scenes so that it can understand what you're saying. RNNs are good at processing audio signals step by step, figuring out the words, the context, and then converting it to something meaningful.

Machine translation (like Google Translate): Think of translating a sentence from English to Japanese, you can't just swap words one by one. RNNs help here by understanding the full sentence structure and meaning, and then generating the translation word-by-word. This makes tools like Google Translate much more accurate and fluent.

Stock market prediction: In finance, past trends often influence future actions, and that's where RNNs come into play. They analyze sequences of stock prices or indicators over time and try to spot patterns. While it's not foolproof (because markets are noisy), they are widely used to make short-term predictions or detect trend changes.

4.5 Why is Deep Learning Becoming So Popular?

The popularity of deep learning has gained a lot of traction, primarily because of its capability to handle complex issues that were previously deemed impossible. Even before we look into some specifics, let's first look at the "Interest over time" from Google Trends for the keyword "Deep Learning" over the last two decades, as shown in Figure 4.17. The trend has been consistently rising.

Figure 4.17 The growing trend of "Deep Learning" on Google

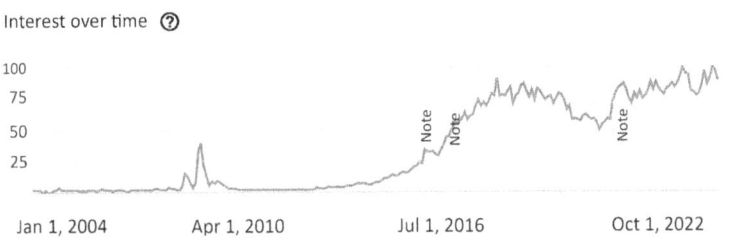

Deep learning models have achieved cutting-edge performance across diverse applications. This includes exceptional performance in areas such as image classification

and natural language processing applications. They have outperformed conventional methods and sometimes even surpassed human experts in certain tasks.

A significant benefit of deep learning, and a crucial factor in grasping its rising popularity, is that it relies on vast quantities of data. The "Big Data Era" of technology offers vast opportunities for fresh innovations in deep learning. According to Andrew Ng, Founder of DeepLearning.AI, "In the analogy of deep learning, the rocket engine represents deep learning models, while the vast amounts of data we provide to these algorithms serve as the fuel."

We can now train these complex deep learning models at low cost. It has become easily accessible through various cloud providers like AWS, Azure, GCP, etc.

Another crucial factor driving the rise of deep learning is its adaptability. These models are being utilized in various domains such as healthcare, finance, retail, automobile, autonomous driving and more. The introduction of transformers and attention mechanisms has further pushed the boundaries of what deep learning can achieve.

Figure 4.18 **Applications of deep learning across industries**

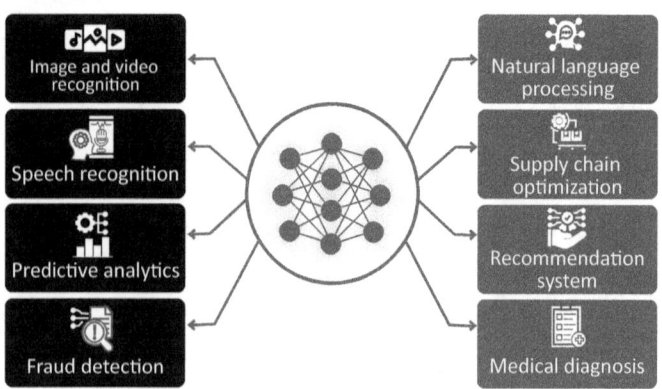

Source: Takyar, A. (2023). What is deep learning, and how does it work? LeewayHertz. https://www.leewayhertz.com/what-is-deep-learning/

4.6 Challenges in Deep Learning

While deep learning offers immense potential, it comes with certain challenges. One of the major challenges in deep learning is overfitting and underfitting, situations in which models learn excessive noise from the training data or do not grasp basic patterns effectively. Additionally, they rely heavily on extensive and high-quality datasets, which are frequently costly and require significant time to obtain and label.

Figure 4.19 Barriers to effective deep learning deployment

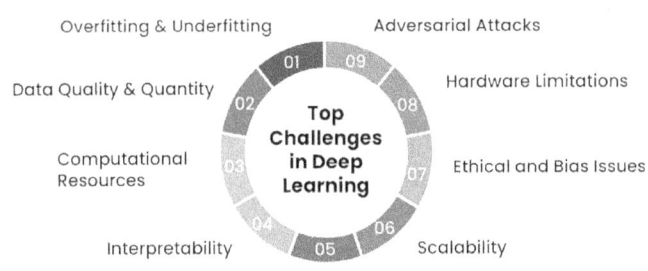

Source: GeeksforGeeks. (2025). Challenges in deep learning. https://www.geeksforgeeks.org/deep-learning/challenges-in-deep-learning/

Deep learning systems also demand significant computational resources, such as GPUs and TPUs, which can limit their accessibility for smaller organizations. Additionally, the opaque nature of these models raises concerns about interpretability, particularly in sectors such as healthcare and finance, where the risks are considerably higher.

Moreover, tuning hyperparameters, achieving scalability, and guaranteeing fairness along with bias reduction remain persistent technical and ethical issues. Finally, adversarial attacks—subtle alterations that can deceive models—continue to pose a significant obstacle to the safe implementation of deep learning in practical applications. Tackling these challenges is crucial for responsibly and effectively scaling deep learning over time.

4.7 Application of Deep Learning Algorithms

Deep learning has transformed industries by enabling AI-driven solutions. These algorithms are powerful and have the capability to solve complex real-world problems. Here are some major applications of deep learning algorithms in various domains:

Healthcare and Life Sciences

- Disease prediction (e.g., identifying malignant cancerous cells from X-rays using CNNs)
- Drug discovery (e.g., predicting how molecules interact with proteins)
- Personalized treatment plans for patients (e.g., recommending tailored cancer treatments based on patient genetics and history)

Retail and E-Commerce

- Demand forecasting (e.g., predicting future product demand using LSTMs to optimize inventory management)
- Supply chain optimization (e.g., using deep reinforcement learning to streamline logistics, reduce delivery times, and cut costs in operations)
- Sentiment analysis (e.g., determining if a social media post is positive or negative)
- Product recommendation engine (e.g., suggesting products based on browsing behavior and past purchases)
- Chatbots and virtual AI assistants (e.g., ChatGPT, Alexa, Siri, and customer support chatbots)

Autonomous Vehicles

- Object detection using CNNs (e.g., identifying traffic signs and pedestrians)
- Route planning using RNNs (e.g., predicting vehicle movements and optimizing routes based on traffic data)
- Sensor fusion using deep reinforcement learning (e.g., combining inputs from radar and cameras to enhance decision-making in self-driving cars)

Finance and Banking

- Credit scoring models using deep neural networks (e.g., assessing a borrower's creditworthiness based on financial history and behavior)
- Anomaly detection for fraudulent transactions (e.g., detecting unusual transaction patterns in credit card usage)
- Algorithmic trading using LSTMs (e.g., predicting stock price movements based on historical data for trading decisions)
- Risk assessment models (e.g., analyzing market trends to assess risks in investment portfolios)

Entertainment Industry

- Netflix and YouTube recommendations using deep learning models (e.g., recommending movies or videos based on user preferences and viewing history)
- Music recommendation on Spotify (e.g., suggesting songs based on listening patterns and user preferences)
- Personalized advertising (e.g., targeting ads to users based on their online behavior and preferences)

Business and Customer Insights

- Customer segmentation (e.g., classifying customers based on purchasing behavior and demographic data for targeted marketing)

- Sales forecasting (e.g., predicting future sales trends to inform inventory and staffing decisions)

- Churn prediction (e.g., predicting customer attrition by analyzing past interactions and engagement with services, like in telecom or subscription-based businesses)

- Dynamic pricing strategies (e.g., optimizing prices based on real-time market demand and competitor pricing)

Let's look at a few of these in detail:

Facial recognition (e.g., Face ID on iPhones): CNNs are trained to identify patterns in faces, starting with simple shapes and edges, and progressing to unique attributes such as eyes and cheekbones. Systems such as FaceNet transform faces into numerical representations, which are subsequently evaluated with similarity metrics such as cosine distance to authenticate and confirm an individual's identity, even amidst different lighting conditions or facial orientations.

Figure 4.20 Deep learning application in facial identification

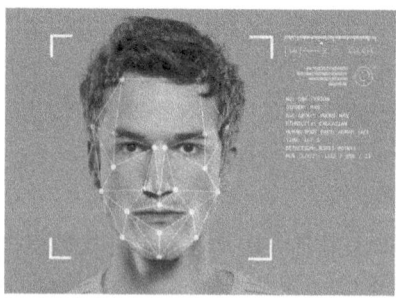

Source: Yadav, R. (2020). 7 best resources to learn facial recognition in 2024. Analytics India Magazine.

Medical imaging (e.g., detecting tumors in MRI scans): In the medical field, CNNs are commonly employed to examine scans such as MRIs, CTs, and X-rays. They assist in detecting irregularities with great precision. Models, such as U-Net, are made for precise segmentation, pinpointing the exact positions of anomalies, such as tumors, at the pixel level. Classifiers are then employed to differentiate between normal and abnormal tissues. These models improve the speed and reliability of diagnoses in comparison to conventional radiological techniques.

Figure 4.21 Brain tumor detection using deep learning

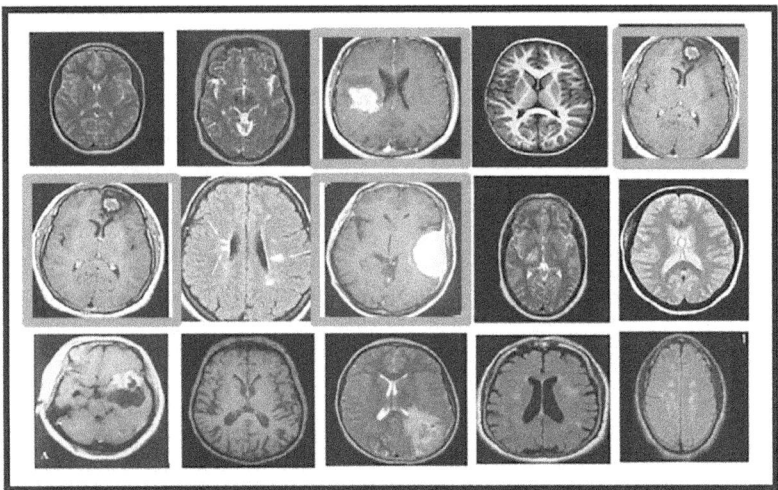

Source: Anantharajan, S., Gunasekaran, S., Subramanian, T., & R, V. (2024). MRI brain tumor detection using deep learning and machine learning approaches. Measurement: Sensors, 31, Article 101026. https://doi.org/10.1016/j.measen.2024.101026

Autonomous vehicles (e.g., identifying pedestrians and traffic signs): They rely majorly on CNNs to understand the surroundings. Models like YOLO help detect pedestrians, signals, markings, etc. This helps in making instant decisions and ensures safe navigation.

Figure 4.22 **CNN-based object detection in road environments**

Source: SuperAnnotate. (2023). Computer vision challenges in autonomous vehicles: The future of AI. SuperAnnotate. https://www.superannotate.com/blog/computer-vision-in-autonomous-vehicles

In conclusion, deep learning has revolutionized AI by enabling machines to learn from vast amounts of data through complex neural networks, paving the way for advanced applications in image recognition, natural language processing, and more. Its continued evolution promises even greater innovations in artificial intelligence.

 **Chapter Summary**

- Deep learning is an extremely useful technique that utilizes neural networks to help algorithms learn from data.

- Deep learning models work by passing data through multiple layers, making predictions, calculating errors, and then iteratively adjusting the model to improve accuracy.

- With CNNs for vision-related problems and RNNs for tasks involving sequential data, deep learning continues to solve complex AI challenges using innovative techniques across various industries.

- Deep learning algorithms are transforming industries through applications in image recognition, natural language processing, and autonomous systems. However, challenges remain, including the need for large datasets, high computational power, and addressing issues like overfitting.

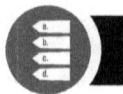 **Quiz**

1. **What does deep learning primarily mimic?**
   a. Statistical analysis
   b. Decision trees
   c. The structure of the human brain
   d. Traditional programming logic

2. **Which of the following is a key characteristic that distinguishes deep learning from traditional machine learning?**
   a. Reliance on manual feature extraction
   b. Use of shallow models
   c. Automatic representation learning through neural networks
   d. Minimal computational requirements

3. **What is one major challenge associated with deep learning compared to traditional ML?**
   a. Lower prediction accuracy
   b. Requirement for large amounts of labeled data
   c. Lack of model complexity
   d. Simpler training processes

4. **What is the primary advantage of representation learning in deep learning?**
   a. It eliminates the need for data cleaning.
   b. It automatically extracts relevant features from data.
   c. It reduces the size of the dataset.
   d. It ensures 100% model interpretability.

5. Which hardware is most commonly used to efficiently train deep learning models?

   a. CPU
   b. FPGA
   c. GPU/TPU
   d. Microcontroller

6. At the heart of deep learning are neural networks. What is the basic structural unit of these networks?

   a. Decision nodes
   b. Neurons
   c. Clusters
   d. Hyperplanes

7. Which process in neural networks is responsible for updating weights by propagating error signals backward?

   a. Forward propagation
   b. Regularization
   c. Backpropagation
   d. Feature scaling

8. Which activation function is most commonly used in deep networks to mitigate the vanishing gradient problem?

   a. Sigmoid
   b. Tanh
   c. ReLU
   d. Softmax

9. **What is the purpose of forward propagation in a neural network?**
   a. To update the model's weights
   b. To send error signals backward
   c. To pass input data through the network to generate output
   d. To normalize the input data

10. **Which type of deep learning network is specifically designed for processing image data?**
    a. Recurrent Neural Network (RNN)
    b. Convolutional Neural Network (CNN)
    c. Feedforward Neural Network
    d. Boltzmann Machine

Answers

1 – c	2 – c	3 – b	4 – b	5 – c
6 – b	7 – c	8 – c	9 – c	10 – b

## CHAPTER 5

Natural Language Processing (NLP)

Key Learning Objectives

- Understand the core concepts of NLP.
- Explore the building blocks of language, such as phonemes, morphemes, syntax, and context, and how they relate to various NLP tasks.
- Learn the end-to-end NLP way of problem-solving which includes data collection, text preprocessing, feature engineering, modeling, evaluation, deployment, and monitoring.
- Understand how advanced techniques like Sentiment Analysis, Named Entity Recognition (NER), and Transformers are used to extract insights and automate language-based tasks.
- Discover real-world applications of NLP across various domains.

Picture this: the CEO of a rapidly growing AI startup kicks off their hectic day by chatting with their digital assistant. In an instant, they get real-time updates on stock market prices and trends, all with just a simple voice command. Sound familiar? We've all interacted with smart assistants like Amazon Alexa, Google Assistant, or Siri to handle similar tasks.

But here's the twist: when we talk to these assistants, we don't use complex coding languages. We speak to them in natural language, the same way we communicate with each other. This ability to speak in our own words is something humans have relied on for centuries, since the very dawn of civilization. Yet, behind the scenes, computers still work in a world of binary, processing everything in 0s and 1s. It's this fascinating blend of human communication and machine logic that makes the world of AI so compelling.

| Figure 5.1 | Natural Language Processing (NLP) in human-computer interaction |

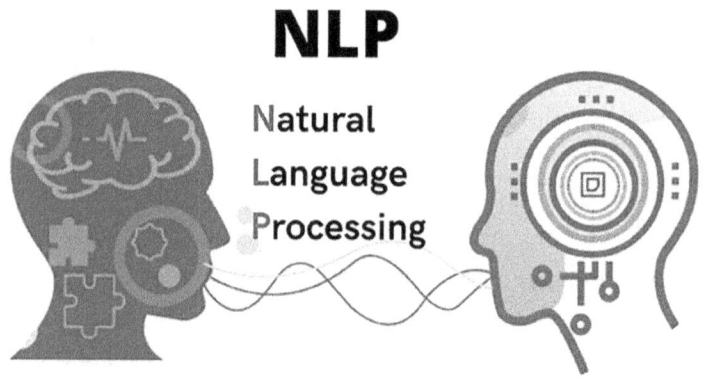

Source: Almacı, A. (2023). NLP (Natural Language Processing) techniques. Stackademic. https://blog.stackademic.com

So, how do we make machines understand the language we speak? That is where Natural Language Processing (NLP) comes in. NLP is a branch of computer science that deals with methods to analyze, model, and understand human language. NLP enables a computer to understand spoken human language as well as written textual content.

Natural language tends to be ambiguous, and the linguistic structure may depend on many complex variables such as slang, regional dialects, and sometimes social context too. Understanding natural languages is difficult for computers because they traditionally require specific instructions expressed in the form of a programming language, which is precise and highly structured.

During my tenure with Alexa, I led the Knowledge AI team for the Australia and New Zealand region. My primary objective was to enhance Alexa's overall intelligence using advanced NLP techniques to improve user engagement. This involved addressing the unique linguistic nuances of Australian and New Zealand English, ensuring that Alexa could understand the accents and respond appropriately to regional dialects. We achieved significant improvements in Alexa's accuracy and responsiveness, making interactions more natural and intuitive. Let's deep-dive into the fundamentals of NLP.

5.1 Fundamentals of NLP

Language is a structured system of communication that involves complex combinations of its constituent components, such as characters, words, sentences, etc. Linguistics is the study of language. To understand NLP, it is very important to grasp a few basic concepts from linguistics.

Human language is composed of four major building blocks:

- Phonemes
- Morphemes and lexemes
- Syntax
- Context

NLP-based applications require knowledge of these different levels, ranging from the basic sounds of (phonemes) to texts with meaningful expressions (context).

5.1.1 Building Blocks of Language

Let us delve deeper into these building blocks to provide context for the challenges involved in NLP.

Figure 5.2 The core components of human language

Source: Adapted from Vajjala, S., Majumder, B., Gupta, A., & Surana, H. (2020). Practical natural language processing: A comprehensive guide to building real-world NLP systems. O'Reilly Media.

Phonemes

Phonemes are the smallest units of sound in a language. They do not have any meaning on their own, but can convey meaning when combined with other phonemes. Phonemes are particularly important in applications which involve speech understanding, such as speech recognition, speech-to-text transcription, and text-to-speech conversion.

Morphemes and Lexemes

A morpheme is the smallest unit of language that has a meaning. It is formed by a combination of phonemes. Not all morphemes are words, but all prefixes and suffixes are morphemes. For example, in the word "multimedia," "multi-" is not a word by itself but a prefix that changes the meaning when put together with "media." Thus, "multi-" is a morpheme. Lexemes are the structural variations of the morphemes that are related to one another by meaning.

For instance, run, runs, ran, and running are different forms of the same lexeme.

Syntax

Syntax is the set of rules that govern how words and phrases are arranged to form grammatically correct sentences in a language. Syntactic structure in linguistics is represented in many ways. A common approach to representing sentences is a parse tree. The syntax of one language can be different from another, and the language-processing approaches needed for that language will also change accordingly.

Context

Context refers to how various parts in a language come together to convey a particular meaning. This includes various long-term references, world knowledge, and common sense, along with the literal meaning of words and phrases. The meaning of a sentence can change based on the context, as sometimes words and phrases can also have multiple meanings. Generally, context is composed of semantics and pragmatics. Semantics refers to the direct meaning of words and sentences without any external context, whereas pragmatics incorporates world knowledge and external context of the conversation, enabling us to infer implied or hidden meaning. Complex NLP tasks such as sarcasm detection, summarization, and topic modelling heavily rely on understanding context.

Now that we have a basic understanding of the building blocks of language, let us explore why language is difficult for computers to understand and what makes NLP such a challenging field.

5.1.2 Why is NLP Challenging?

The ambiguity and creativity of human language are two key characteristics that make the field of NLP particularly challenging.

Ambiguity: Ambiguity refers to the uncertainty of meaning. Most languages are inherently ambiguous. For instance, the sentence "She passed it to him" could refer to handing over a toy in a story about a mother and child, but in a sports book, it might describe a player passing a ball to a teammate. The words are the same, but the interpretation changes based on the situation. These are examples of direct ambiguity. When it comes to idioms or figurative expressions, the level of ambiguity increases significantly.

Creativity: Language is not only rule-driven, but it also involves a creative aspect. Various styles, dialects, genres, and variations are used in any language. Poetry is the best example of creativity in language. Teaching machines to understand this creativity is a difficult problem, not just in NLP, but in AI as a whole.

For most of the languages in the world, there is no direct mapping between the vocabularies of any two languages. This makes it difficult to adapt an NLP solution developed for one language to another. This means that one either builds a solution that is language-neutral or language-specific. While the first one is extremely difficult, the latter is manual and time-intensive. Having worked with the Alexa NLP and the AI team at Amazon, I've seen firsthand how challenging NLP can be, yet it's precisely these challenges that make the work so rewarding.

These challenges show why NLP cannot rely on a single, universal approach. Instead, solving NLP problems requires a systematic process that breaks down the complexity of language into manageable steps. This is where the concept of an NLP project pipeline becomes essential.

5.2 NLP Project Pipeline

We use NLP applications in our day-to-day activities. But if we were asked to build such an application, how would we approach it? We would break the entire process into several sub-processes and solve them. Since language processing is involved, we would apply various forms of text processing at each stage. This step-by-step processing of text is known as a pipeline. A pipeline is a series of steps involved in building any NLP model. In this section, we will explore the various stages of the NLP pipeline.

The key stages in the NLP project pipeline are:

Figure 5.3 Stages in the NLP project pipeline

```
┌─────────────────┐    ┌───────────────┐    ┌─────────────────┐    ┌──────────────────┐
│ Data collection │ ─→ │ Text cleaning │ ─→ │ Pre-processing  │ ─→ │     Feature      │
│                 │    │               │    │                 │    │   engineering    │
└─────────────────┘    └───────────────┘    └─────────────────┘    └──────────────────┘
                                                                             │
                                                                             ↓
┌─────────────────┐    ┌───────────────┐    ┌─────────────────┐    ┌──────────────────┐
│   Monitoring    │ ←─ │  Deployment   │ ←─ │   Evaluation    │ ←─ │    Modelling     │
└─────────────────┘    └───────────────┘    └─────────────────┘    └──────────────────┘
```

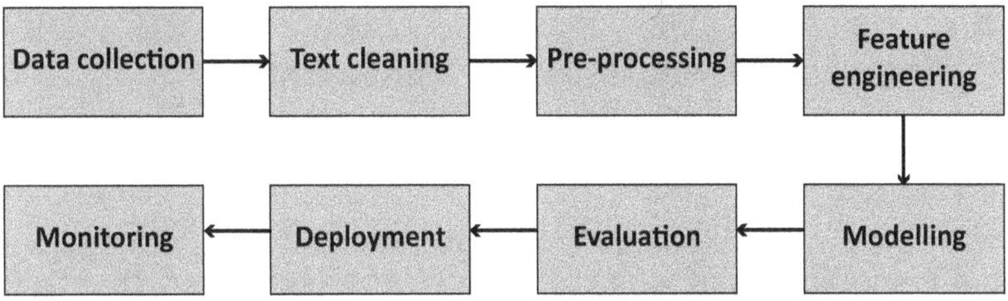

5.2.1 Data Collection

Data is at the heart of any ML system. In most industrial projects, data often becomes the bottleneck. Therefore, gathering relevant data for an NLP project is important. Ideally, we want labelled data, a collection of queries where each one is labelled with *sales* or *support*. But how can we obtain such data?

- **Use a publicly available dataset:** We can start by looking for public datasets that we can leverage. If you find a suitable dataset that matches the task at hand, great! You can build a model and evaluate it. But what if we don't find a suitable dataset?

- **Scrape data:** We could look for relevant data sources on the internet, for example, a consumer or discussion forum where people have posted queries related to sales or support. We can scrape the data from there and have it labelled by human annotators.

For many industrial settings, gathering data from external sources does not suffice because the data doesn't contain nuances like product names or product-specific user behavior, making it very different from what is seen in production environments. In such cases, we need to start looking for data within the organization.

5.2.2 Text Extraction and Cleanup

Text extraction and cleanup refer to the process of extracting raw text from input data by removing all the other non-textual information, such as markup, metadata, etc., and converting the text to the required encoding format. For example, when working with customer support emails exported from a helpdesk system, each message might include HTML tags, timestamps, and auto-generated footers. All of this noise must be cleaned up to extract only the meaningful message.

Text extraction is a standard data-wrangling step, and we don't usually employ any NLP-specific techniques during this process. However, in my experience, it is an important step that has implications for all other aspects of the NLP pipeline. Further, it can also be the most time-consuming part of a project.

5.2.3 Pre-Processing

Our text extraction step removed all extraneous content and gave us the plain text of the article we needed. However, all NLP software typically works at the sentence level and expects a separation of words, at the very least. So, we need a method to split a text into words and sentences before proceeding further.

Sometimes, we need to remove special characters and digits; other times, we may choose to convert all words to lowercase if case is not important. Many more decisions like this are made while processing the text. Such decisions are addressed during the pre-processing step of the NLP pipeline.

Here are some common preprocessing steps used in NLP software:

- **Preliminaries:** NLP software typically analyses text by breaking it up into words (tokens) and sentences. Hence, any NLP pipeline must start with a reliable system to split the text into sentences (sentence segmentation) and further split a sentence into words (word tokenization).

- **Sentence tokenization:** It involves breaking up text into sentences, typically at punctuation marks like full stops and question marks. However, there may be abbreviations, forms of addresses (e.g., Dr., Mr., etc.), or ellipses (...) that may break this simple rule.

  For example, given the paragraph:

  "Beauty lies in the eyes of the beholder. Do not open your eyes. A thing of beauty is a joy forever."

  After sentence tokenization, the following list of sentences will be generated:

```
['Beauty lies in the eyes of the beholder.',
'Do not open your eyes.',
'A thing of beauty is a joy forever.']
```

- **Word tokenization:** Similar to sentence tokenization, word tokenization refers to splitting a sentence into individual words. A simple rule might be to split text based on spaces and punctuation marks. This preprocessing task is supported by most NLP libraries (e.g. NLTK, StanfordCoreNLP, OpenNLP, etc.)

  For example, given the sentence:

  "A quick brown fox jumps over the lazy dogs."

  After word tokenization, the following list of words will be generated:

```
['A', 'quick', 'brown', 'fox', 'jumps', 'over', 'the',
'lazy', 'dogs', '.']
```

- **Stemming:** Stemming refers to the process of removing suffixes and reducing a word to its base form, such that all different variants of that word can be represented by the same form. This is accomplished by applying a fixed set of rules. The resulting form of the word after stemming is known as the stem or root word.

  For example:

  adjustments → adjust.

- **Lemmatization:** Lemmatization also reduces words to their base form, or lemma, but unlike stemming, it uses a vocabulary and considers the context and part of speech of the word. This typically results in more accurate base forms.

For example:

- ○ am, are, is → be
- ○ car, cars, car's, cars' → car

- **Text normalization:** A word can be spelled in different ways, including shortened forms; a phone number can be written in different formats (e.g., with or without hyphens); names are sometimes in lowercase, and so on. When we're developing NLP tools to work with such data, it's useful to reach a canonical representation of text that captures all these variations into one representation. This process of standardizing text into a consistent format is known as text normalization.

5.2.4 Feature Engineering

Feature engineering involves transforming raw text data into meaningful features. The goal of feature engineering is to represent the characteristics of the text as numeric vectors that can be understood by the ML algorithms, which enhances the model performance.

5.2.5 Modeling

We now have some amount of data related to our NLP project and a clear idea of what sort of cleaning up and pre-processing needs to be done, and what features need to be extracted. The next step is to build a useful solution using this data.

Initially, when we have limited data, we can use simpler methods and rule-based approaches. Over time, with more data and a better understanding of the problem, we can add more complexity to improve performance. For text-based models, we can use traditional ML algorithms like Naive Bayes, Support Vector Machines (SVMs), or opt for deep learning models like Recurrent Neural Networks (RNNs) or Long Short-Term Memory networks (LSTMs).

5.2.6 Evaluation

A key step in the NLP pipeline is to measure how good the model we've built is. The "goodness" of a model can have multiple meanings, but the most common interpretation is the measure of the model's performance on unseen data. Success in this phase depends on two factors:

Using the Right Metric for Evaluation

Different NLP tasks require different evaluation metrics. Choosing an incorrect metric can lead to misleading interpretations of model performance.

For example, let's say for a classification task (like sentiment analysis), the most common metrics include accuracy, precision, recall and F1 score. In cases of imbalanced datasets, accuracy alone cannot be reliable. A model predicting "not spam" for everything will show 95% accuracy, but chances are that it will completely fail in practice. In such scenarios, precision and recall are more meaningful.

For sequence generation tasks (like machine translation), metrics like BLEU (Bilingual Evaluation Understudy Score), ROUGE (Recall-Oriented Understudy for Gisting Evaluation), and METEOR (Metric for Evaluation of Translation with Explicit ORdering) are used to measure how close the generated text is to a reference. These metrics are essential as assessing generated text is subjective, and it is not as simple as classification. Each metric assists in measuring how "similar" the machine-generated sequence is to a human-written reference, allowing for more uniform and automated assessment of these tasks.

Lastly, for tasks like topic modeling or embeddings, other metrics such as coherence scores, silhouette scores, or intrinsic evaluations using word similarity tasks are more relevant.

The key is aligning the metric with the business objective. For example, a customer service chatbot might prioritize precision over recall to avoid giving incorrect advice, even if that means fewer questions are answered.

Following the Right Evaluation Process

Using the right metric is important, but so is using the right evaluation method. Evaluation isn't just about achieving a high score; it's about ensuring that the model performs well in real-world settings. Let's look at some commonly used evaluation approaches:

- **Train-test split:** Bifurcates the dataset into training and test sets so that the model is evaluated on data it hasn't seen before. However, results may vary depending on how the split is performed.

- **Stratified sampling:** Ensures that the distribution of classes in each fold or split is similar to the overall distribution, which is crucial for tasks with imbalanced data.

- **Cross-validation:** A more robust method in which the dataset is divided into k-folds (e.g., 5 or 10), and the model is trained and evaluated multiple times, each time with a different test fold. This helps reduce variance and ensures the model's performance is more generalized.

- **Confusion matrix analysis:** Provides a detailed breakdown of true positives, false positives, true negatives, and false negatives, offering insights into where the model is making errors.

5.2.7 Deployment

Deployment entails plugging the NLP module into the broader system. It may also involve ensuring that input and output data pipelines are in order, as well as making sure the NLP module is scalable under heavy load.

It also requires setting up supporting components like:

- **Input and output data pipelines:** Ensures the system can feed the model clean, appropriately formatted text and interpret its outputs correctly.

- **APIs or microservices:** Exposes the model's functionality to other parts of the application (e.g., web or mobile frontends).

- **Monitoring systems:** Tracks model performance in real-time and detects drift or errors post-deployment.

Key Caveats to Consider

- **Input Format Dependency:** Most NLP models expect inputs in a very specific format, like preprocessed tokens, fixed-length sequences, or text encoded using particular tokenizers. Any deviation in input structure during inference (e.g., raw or noisy text from users) can significantly impact model performance. Therefore, the preprocessing steps used during training must be consistently applied during production.

- **Integration Challenges:** Integrating NLP models into legacy systems or existing applications isn't always easy. These systems may have been built without NLP in mind, and could require significant refactoring (like adapters or wrappers) to share data correctly to and from the model.

- **Latency and Scalability:** NLP models can be computationally intensive. In customer-facing applications (like chatbots or real-time sentiment analysis), latency becomes an important parameter to consider. Optimizations such as quantization (making the model use smaller numbers), distillation (training a smaller model from a big one), or simply choosing lighter models can be handy. Likewise, deployment needs to account for scalability, especially under high traffic, which might involve running models inside containers (like Docker), organizing them with tools (like Kubernetes), and adding more machines when needed (horizontal scaling).

- **Security and Privacy:** If the NLP module processes sensitive user data (emails, feedback, chats), it must comply with data privacy regulations like the General Data Protection Regulation (GDPR) or the Health Insurance Portability and Accountability Act (HIPAA). Data retention policies and encryption mechanisms need to be considered during deployment.

In essence, deployment is not just the "last step" in the pipeline, but a phase that bridges the gap between theory and real-world impact. It tests the robustness of everything built so far, from preprocessing to modeling, under the constraints of production systems and user expectations.

5.2.8 Monitoring and Model Updating

Monitoring for NLP projects and models must be handled differently from a regular engineering project, as we need to ensure that the outputs produced by our models each day make sense. If the model is being retrained automatically on a frequent basis, we must make sure that the models behave in a reasonable manner. Once the model is deployed and begins gathering new data, it should be iteratively updated with this data to keep its predictions current and reliable.

Effective monitoring helps ensure that NLP models remain accurate and reliable in production. However, building models that can truly understand complex language patterns requires architectures capable of capturing nuanced context. This brings us to Transformers, a breakthrough in deep learning for NLP.

5.3 Transformers

Transformers are the latest entry in the league of deep learning models for NLP. Transformer models have achieved state-of-the-art results in almost all major NLP tasks in the past couple of years. They model the textual context, but not in a sequential manner. Given a word in the input, they consider all the words around it and represent each word with respect to its context. For example, the word "bank" has different meanings depending on the context in which it appears. If the context talks about finance, then "bank" probably denotes a financial institution. On the other hand, if the context mentions a river, it probably indicates the bank of the river. Transformers can model such context and hence have been used heavily in NLP tasks due to their higher representation capacity as compared to other deep networks.

Recently, large transformers have been used for transfer learning on smaller downstream tasks. Transfer learning is a technique in AI where the knowledge gained while solving one problem is applied to a different but related problem. With transformers, the idea is to train a very large transformer model in an unsupervised manner (known as pre-training) to predict parts of a sentence given the rest, so that it can encode the high-level nuances of language. These models are trained on more than 40 GB of textual data, scraped from the whole internet. An example of a large transformer is BERT (Bidirectional Encoder Representations from transformers), which is pre-trained on massive data and open-sourced by Google.

Due to the sheer amount of pre-trained knowledge, BERT works efficiently in transferring the knowledge for downstream tasks and achieves state-of-the-art performance in many of them.

5.3.1 Why Transformers?

Traditional NLP models like RNNs and LSTMs process words sequentially, which limits the efficiency and ability to capture long-range dependencies. However, transformers process input in parallel, eliminate recurrence, and use self-attention to model relationships between all tokens in a sequence, irrespective of their position.

The transformer architecture, introduced in the paper *"Attention Is All You Need"* by Vaswani et al. (2017), eliminates the need for recurrence by using self-attention and encoding. This makes transformers highly effective for sequence-to-sequence tasks such as language translation and text generation.

5.3.2 Transformer Architecture

A transformer model basically consists of two main components: an encoder and a decoder. Both are built using many layers of self-attention, which allows them to weigh the relevance of different words in a sentence simultaneously, regardless of their position and feedforward networks.

The encoder is responsible for reading the input and generating representations, while the decoder takes the output from the encoder and creates predictions.

Figure 5.4 Sample transformer architecture

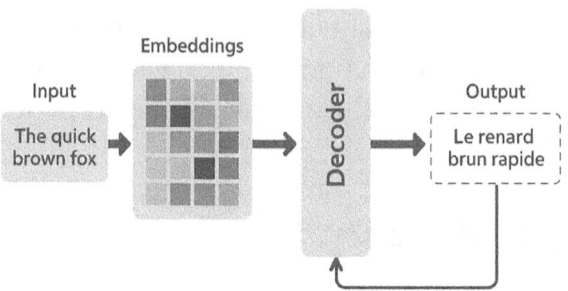

Source: Great Learning Editorial Team. (2025). What is transformer architecture and how it works? Great Learning. https://www.mygreatlearning.com/blog/understanding-transformer-architecture/

Let's understand the encoder and decoder in detail.

Encoder

The encoder takes the input text and transforms it into a continuous representation. Each encoder block contains:

(a) Self-attention layer, which helps the model weigh the importance of other words in the input.

(b) Feedforward Neural Network (FNN), which applies non-linearity and transformations on each token's representation.

(c) Residual connections and layer normalization, which helps in training deeper models by avoiding vanishing gradients.

Decoder

The decoder takes the encoder's representation and generates the output text. Each decoder block contains:

(a) Masked self-attention, which ensures predictions are made one step at a time (especially important in text generation).

(b) Encoder-decoder attention, which helps the decoder focus on relevant parts of the input sequence.

(c) Feedforward network, residual connections, and layer normalization, which is similar to encoder.

5.3.3 The Self-Attention Mechanism

The self-attention mechanism is the core of the transformer. It allows the model to assign weights to each word in a sentence relative to every other word. This is particularly powerful in understanding relationships across long texts. Given a set of input embeddings, the model creates:

- Query (Q): What the model is looking for.
- Key (K): What each word offers.
- Value (V): The actual content.

The attention score is then computed to determine how much focus each word should place on others when forming its contextual representation.

5.3.4 Transfer Learning with Transformers

One of the most powerful aspects of transformers is their ability to leverage transfer learning. It mainly involves two steps: pre-training and fine-tuning. The model is trained on huge amounts of unlabelled text to understand language constructs.

For instance, BERT is trained on over 40 GB of text data, allowing it to learn complex language representations. The pre-trained model is then fine-tuned on specific, smaller datasets for downstream tasks such as text classification, entity extraction, question answering, etc.

Key Transformer Models

- **BERT (Bidirectional Encoder Representations from Transformers):** Performs well in understanding the context of words in all directions.

- **GPT (Generative Pre-trained Transformer):** Specializes in text generation, powering applications like chatbots and content creation.

- **T5 (Text-To-Text Transfer Transformer):** Converts all NLP tasks into a text-to-text format, thus, streamlining the problem-solving approach.

- **RoBERTa (Robustly Optimized BERT):** An optimized variant of BERT with more training data and computation.

Transformers have revolutionized NLP tasks like language translation, text summarization, chatbots, and virtual assistants. In the next section, we will understand the various applications of NLP.

5.4 Applications of NLP

There is a wide variety of NLP applications that use data from social platforms, including sentiment detection, customer support, and opinion mining, to name a few. This section will briefly discuss some of the popular use-cases of NLP to provide an idea of where we could begin applying these techniques, for example, trending topic detection, sentiment analysis, fake news detection, and customer support. In particular, we will focus on understanding the applications of NLP in detail for Sentiment Analysis and Named Entity Recognition (NER).

5.4.1 Sentiment Analysis

Sentiment analysis, which is also called opinion mining, is the field of study that analyzes people's opinions, sentiments, appraisals, attitudes, and emotions toward entities and their attributes as expressed in written text. These entities can be products, services, organizations, individuals, events, issues, or topics. The field represents a large problem space. Terms like sentiment analysis, opinion mining, opinion analysis, opinion extraction, sentiment mining, subjectivity analysis, affect analysis, emotion analysis, and review mining, are often used interchangeably and all fall under the broader umbrella of 'sentiment analysis'.

Figure 5.5 **Visualizing sentiment from negative to positive**

Sentences expressing opinions or sentiments are usually subjective (reflecting personal feelings or judgments), in contrast to objective sentences (stating facts). However, objective sentences can imply positive or negative sentiments of their authors too, because they may describe desirable or undesirable facts. For example, "I bought the car yesterday and it broke down today," and "after sleeping on the mattress for a month, a valley has formed in the middle" describe two undesirable facts. We can safely infer that both sentences clearly suggest negative experiences. Sentiment analysis studies such objective sentences as well.

In a nutshell, sentiment analysis aims to identify positive and negative opinions or sentiments expressed or implied in text and determine the targets of these opinions.

Over the years, social media systems have provided excellent platforms to facilitate and enable audience participation, engagement, and community, which has resulted in a new participatory culture. From reviews and blogs to YouTube, Facebook, and Twitter (now X), people have enthusiastically embraced these platforms because they enable their users to freely and conveniently voice their opinions and communicate their views on any subject across geographic and spatial boundaries. Amazon would build similar sentiment analysis over customer feedback about products and display it on the website as well, which would help customers make an informed decision before buying any product online.

Here's a basic example of performing sentiment analysis using Python's NLTK library, and let's understand how it works under the hood:

```python
import nltk
from nltk.sentiment import SentimentIntensityAnalyzer
# Download the VADER lexicon
nltk.download('vader_lexicon')
# Initialize the sentiment analyzer
sia = SentimentIntensityAnalyzer()
# Sample text
text = "I absolutely love the new design of your website!"
# Perform sentiment analysis
score = sia.polarity_scores(text)

# Output the results - Positive, Negative & Neutral along
with the scores.
print(f"Sentiment Scores: {score}")
Sentiment Scores: {'neg': 0.0, 'neu': 0.254, 'pos': 0.746,
'compound': 0.8519}
```

How Does This Work Behind the Scenes?

The `SentimentIntensityAnalyzer` in NLTK uses **VADER** (Valence Aware Dictionary for Sentiment Reasoning), which is a lexicon and rule-based sentiment analysis tool specifically tuned for social media text and general-purpose sentiment tasks. Here's a breakdown of how VADER processes a sentence:

Lexicon-based scoring: Each word in the sentence is looked up in the VADER lexicon, which contains a dictionary of words (e.g., "love", "hate", "great") tagged to sentiment scores ranging from -4 (most negative) to +4 (most positive).

In the example sentence - "I absolutely love the new design of your website!"

- The word "love" has a strong positive valence in the VADER dictionary.
- To add to it, words like "absolutely" are intensifiers, which boosts the sentiment of the following word.

Heuristics and rules: VADER applies a set of heuristics to modify base sentiment scores:

- Degree modifiers: Words like *very*, *extremely*, or *absolutely* increase intensity.
- Negations: Words like *not* or *isn't* flip polarity.
- Punctuation and capitalization: Exclamation marks (!) and ALL CAPS can amplify sentiment.

So, in *"I absolutely love the new design of your website!"*:

- "Love" has a strong positive score.
- "Absolutely" boosts that score further.
- The exclamation mark amplifies the final sentiment.

Score aggregation: The analyzer then combines the adjusted scores to produce:

- pos: Probability of positive sentiment
- neu: Probability of neutrality
- neg: Probability of negative sentiment
- compound: A normalized, weighted sum of all scores between -1 (most negative) and +1 (most positive)

In this case, the compound score of 0.8519 indicates a *strongly positive sentiment.*

5.4.2 Named Entity Recognition (NER)

Consider a scenario where a user types the search query "Where was Albert Einstein born?" using the Google search. The search engine returns a list of results and highlights "Ulm, Germany." To do this, the system first needs to recognize that Albert Einstein is a person before looking up his place of birth. This is an example of NER in action in a real-world application.

Figure 5.6 **Sample NER view**

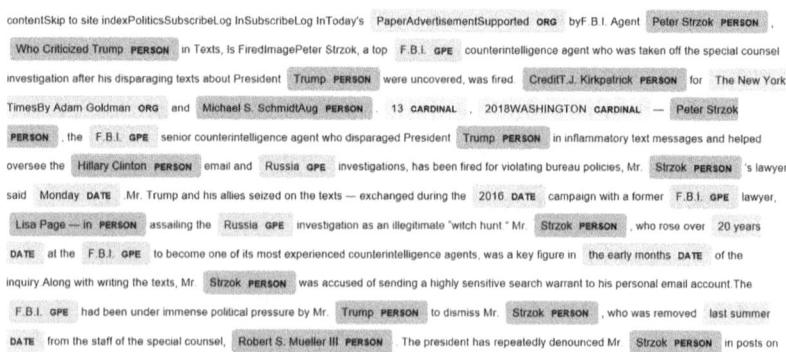

Source: Wisecube. (2023). Named Entity Recognition (NER) with Python. Wisecube.

NER refers to the task of identifying entities in a document. Entities are typically names of persons, locations, and organizations, but they may also include specialized strings, such as monetary expressions, dates, products, names/numbers of laws or articles, and so on. NER is an important step in the pipeline of several NLP applications involving information extraction.

Some common types of named entities include:

- **People** - name of a person e.g: *Steve Jobs* or *Bill Gates*
- **Organizations** - name of a company, organization, or an institution, such as *Amazon* or *Harvard University*
- **Locations** - name of places, such as *India*, *Germany*, *Mount Fuji*
- **Products** - name of items, such as *Macbook* or *Pepsi*
- **Events** - name of events, such as *Superbowl* or *Olympics*

For a given text, NER is expected to identify people, locations, dates, and other entities. These categories are commonly used in NER system development. NER is a prerequisite for more advanced information extraction (IE) tasks such as relation extraction or event extraction. It also has direct applications in areas like machine translation, where names often remain untranslated. Clearly, NER plays a key role in a wide range of NLP projects and is one of the most common tasks in industry applications.

A named entity can be thought of as a "real-world object" that is assigned a name, for example, a person, a place, a country, a product, etc. Using a python library called spaCy (https://spacy.io/), it can recognize various types of named entities in a document by asking the model for predictions. Named entities are available as the `ents` property of a Doc.

The Python NLP library spaCy provides pre-trained NER models like `en_core_web_sm`, which use a combination of word embeddings, transition-based parsing, and statistical classification to predict named entities.

Here's a simple example:

```
import spacy
nlp = spacy.load("en_core_web_sm")
doc = nlp("Apple is looking at buying U.K. startup for $1
billion")
for ent in doc.ents:
    print(ent.text, ent.start_char, ent.end_char, ent.
label_)
```

Output:

```
Apple 0 5 ORG
U.K. 27 31 GPE
$1 billion 44 54 MONEY
```

Apple (characters 0–5) is recognized as an ORG (organization). U.K. (characters 27–31) is recognized as a GPE (geo-political entity). $1 billion (characters 44–54) is recognized as MONEY.

Under the hood, the en_core_web_sm model is trained on the OntoNotes 5 corpus and uses a pipeline of NLP components, including a tagger, parser, and NER. The NER component is a statistical model that predicts a sequence of tags for each token in the document.

A more practical approach to NER is to train an ML model that predicts named entities in unseen text. For each word, a decision must be made whether that word is an entity, and if it is, what type it belongs to. Unlike standard classifiers (e.g., sentiment analysis models) that treat each input independently, NER is a sequence labeling problem, meaning, predictions depend on the surrounding context. Consider a classifier that classifies sentences in a movie review into positive/negative/neutral categories based on their sentiment. This classifier does not (usually) take into account the sentiment of previous (or subsequent) sentences when classifying the current sentence.

A common use case for sequence labelling is part-of-speech (POS) tagging, where we need information about the parts of speech of surrounding words to estimate the part of speech of the current word. Similarly, NER is traditionally modeled as a sequence classification problem, where the prediction for the current word depends on its context.

NLP enables machines to process and understand human language by recognizing patterns, structure, and context in text. From tagging parts of speech to identifying named entities, you've seen how models can extract meaningful information from raw language data.

Now that you've explored how machines handle text, it's time to look at how they interpret images. In the next chapter, we'll dive into Computer Vision, the field focused on teaching machines to see, analyze, and understand the visual world.

Chapter Summary

- NLP enables machines to understand and interact with human language, both spoken and written, despite the complexity, ambiguity, and creativity of natural communication.

- At its core, NLP relies on four building blocks— phonemes (sounds), morphemes/lexemes (meaning units), syntax (grammar), and semantics and pragmatics (context)—each essential for tasks like speech recognition, parsing, and disambiguation.

- The chapter walks through the full NLP pipeline, right from data extraction to model building, deployment, and monitoring.

- Transformer-based models like BERT and GPT have dramatically improved performance in language understanding by modeling context more effectively and supporting transfer learning across diverse tasks.

- Practical applications such as sentiment analysis and Named Entity Recognition (NER) showcase how NLP is used in real-world scenarios.

 **Quiz**

1. **What is the main purpose of tokenization in NLP?**
   a. To translate text into another language
   b. To split text into smaller pieces like words or sentences
   c. To remove stop words from text
   d. To generate word embeddings

2. **Which of the following is not one of the core components of human language?**
   a. Syntax
   b. Phoneme
   c. Transformer
   d. Context

3. **What is a morpheme in the context of linguistics?**
   a. The smallest unit of meaning in a language
   b. A complete sentence with meaning
   c. A rule for sentence structure
   d. The tone in which a word is spoken

4. **In NLP, which method is used to group similar words with the same root?**
   a. Tokenization
   b. Lemmatization
   c. Stemming
   d. Vectorization

5. **What is the main difference between stemming and lemmatization?**

    a. Lemmatization is faster than stemming
    b. Stemming provides the root form, while lemmatization provides the dictionary form
    c. Stemming is more accurate than lemmatization
    d. Both are exactly the same

6. **In an NLP pipeline, what is the main purpose of preprocessing?**

    a. To deploy the model to production
    b. To collect data from the internet
    c. To generate images from text
    d. To clean and structure the raw text data

7. **Which of the following models is an example of a transformer-based architecture?**

    a. Naive Bayes
    b. LSTM
    c. BERT
    d. SVM

8. **What does the "self-attention" mechanism in transformers help with?**

    a. Compressing text
    b. Ignoring irrelevant sentences
    c. Translating numerical data to text
    d. Identifying the relationship between all words in a sentence

9. In Sentiment Analysis, what does a high "compound" score (e.g., 0.85) indicate?
   a. Strongly positive sentiment
   b. Neutral sentiment
   c. Strongly negative sentiment
   d. Lack of data

10. Which NLP task involves identifying entities like names, dates, and locations in text?
   a. Lemmatization
   b. Stemming
   c. NER
   d. Text classification

Answers

1 – b	2 – c	3 – a	4 – c	5 – b
6 – d	7 – c	8 – d	9 – a	10 – c

## CHAPTER 6

Computer Vision (CV)

Key Learning Objectives

- Understand the core concepts of computer vision, including image classification, object detection, and semantic segmentation.
- Explore advanced techniques like YOLO and GANs for real-time object detection and image generation.
- Learn the process of feature extraction, object tracking, and pattern identification in visual data.
- Discover real-world applications of computer vision in healthcare, autonomous vehicles, agriculture, and surveillance.
- Examine popular computer vision platforms like OpenCV and TensorFlow for hands-on implementation.

6.1 Introduction and Evolution of Computer Vision

Have you ever wondered how your smartphone unlocks solely by recognizing your face? Or how Snapchat filters can quickly transform you into a dog, cat, or even a cartoon character? Or how do Tesla's autonomous vehicles maneuver through roads with impressive accuracy?

Computer Vision (CV) allows machines to analyze and comprehend the visual world. From real-time object recognition to producing hyperrealistic visuals, it is being adopted across sectors such as healthcare, automotive, security, and manufacturing. But what exactly happens behind the scenes? And in what ways is it influencing the tools and technologies we utilize daily?

Let's understand CV in detail and figure out how machines are acquiring the ability to "see" much like humans.

Computer vision is a field within AI that focuses on enabling computers to walk through and understand the visual world, much like how humans do in this digital age, where most of our consumption is either of images or videos. Given a two-dimensional image, a computer vision system must recognize the present objects and their characteristics, such as shapes, textures, colors, sizes, spatial arrangements, among other things to provide a comprehensive description of the image.

Figure 6.1 **How AI and computer vision systems process data**

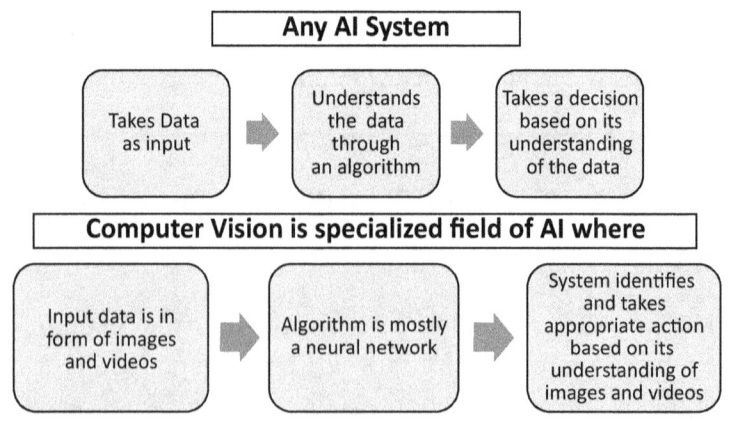

The evolution of computer vision has been nothing short of remarkable. Think about it, just two decades ago, the field was still finding its footing. Then came the breakthrough moment: deep learning algorithms emerged, and CNNs began transforming how machines could process images. Computer vision transformed self-driving cars from science fiction into a reality on roads. These vehicles began to "see" the world around them, spotting obstacles and finding their way through complex environments.

In the last decade, YOLO technology ("You Only Look Once") revolutionized how computers could identify objects in real-time. Meanwhile, facial recognition has become so sophisticated that we barely think twice when unlocking our phones with just a glance.

Looking ahead, we're likely to see computer vision become even more seamlessly integrated into our daily routines. Real-time recognition will likely become more accurate, autonomous vehicles will rely on increasingly sophisticated visual systems, and healthcare applications could revolutionize early diagnosis. Don't be surprised if your home gets a bit smarter too, with everyday objects that can "see" and respond to your needs.

6.1.1 How Does Computer Vision Work

Computer vision enables machines to analyze and interpret visual data, much like humans. It uses a combination of cameras, sensors, and AI algorithms trained on huge amounts of visual information to make sense of the world. This ability has driven innovation across sectors from healthcare and manufacturing to security, retail, and autonomous vehicles.

| Figure 6.2 | Real-time detection using computer vision |

Let's break down the key steps that occur in a typical computer vision pipeline:

- **Capture the image:** The process begins when a camera, or a scanner, captures an image or video frame. This visual data, that is raw, serves as the input to computer vision algorithms.

- **Interpret the image:** Once the image is captured, AI-powered systems process the data to detect and recognize patterns. These systems compare the image content against large databases which might include known objects, facial features, or even medical scan references to identify what's in the frame.

- **Analyze data:** The AI system then uses what it has learned to understand the image by spotting people, objects, defects, symptoms, or anomalies depending on the context. For instance, in a factory, it might detect a missing screw in a machine part; in a hospital, it could flag a potential tumor in an X-ray.

- **Deliver insights:** Finally, the AI system outputs actionable insights. These might trigger automated responses (like stopping a machine), alert a human (such as notifying a doctor), or even help companies better understand customer behavior via in-store analytics.

This entire process is made possible by the deep learning revolution, especially through models known as convolutional neural networks (CNNs). While traditional algorithms can identify simple features like edges or colors, they struggle to understand what they're actually looking at. That's where CNNs step in: a specialized class of deep learning models that mimic how the human visual system processes images.

We have already explored CNNs in detail in Chapter 4, covering concepts like convolutional layers, filters, pooling, and flattening, which serve as the foundational engine behind many modern computer vision applications. Hence, we will not revisit CNNs here. Instead, let's focus on the remaining key components of computer vision.

Let's walk through a common application: image classification. Look at Figure 6.3. You can easily distinguish between a dog or a cat. But how would an AI system classify the same image?

Figure 6.3 **CNN-based image classification example**

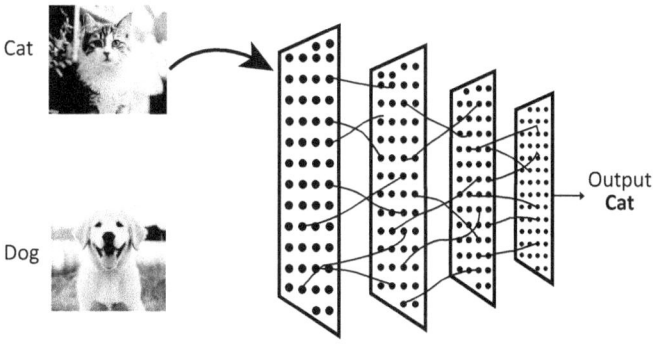

To summarize, here's how a CNN would approach this task:

- **Input layer:** The image is converted into pixel values, where a grid of numbers represents RGB color intensities.

- **Convolutional layers:** Filters are applied to detect basic patterns like edges and textures. Deeper layers recognize more complex structures like ears, tails, or fur.

- **Pooling layers:** These reduce the spatial size of the image while retaining key features, helping the model become faster and more generalizable.

- **Fully connected layers:** The features are combined to form a prediction.

- **Output layer:** The model outputs probabilities — for example, 90% cat, 10% dog — and chooses the most likely result.

Over time, and with enough training data, CNNs learn which features matter most, becoming highly accurate at interpreting new, unseen images. This architecture powers everything from real-time pedestrian detection in self-driving cars to MRI scans in modern healthcare—giving machines a structured way to "see" the world.

6.2 Key Components of Computer Vision

Some common methods used in machine vision include AI-based pattern recognition, feature extraction, and image processing. Computer vision applications run on algorithms that are trained on massive amounts of visual data in the cloud. These algorithms learn to recognize patterns in the data and use them to determine the content of new images.

6.2.1 Feature Extraction

In machine learning and data analysis, feature extraction is an essential step. Before training, raw data must be carefully selected and transformed to produce features that are well-suited for modeling. During this phase, the system checks the incoming visual data to identify and segregate important visual components, such as edges, shapes, textures, and patterns. These features play an important role because they serve as the building blocks for later stages of analysis. To facilitate computation, these mined features are translated into numerical representations, effectively converting visual information into a format that machines can comprehend and process more efficiently. The machine performs the following operations:

- **Represent colors by numbers:** In computer science, each color can be represented numerically (e.g., by RGB values or a hexadecimal code). This is how machines interpret the colors that make up image pixels, whereas humans intuitively perceive and distinguish shades.

Figure 6.4	How computers represent colors using numeric values

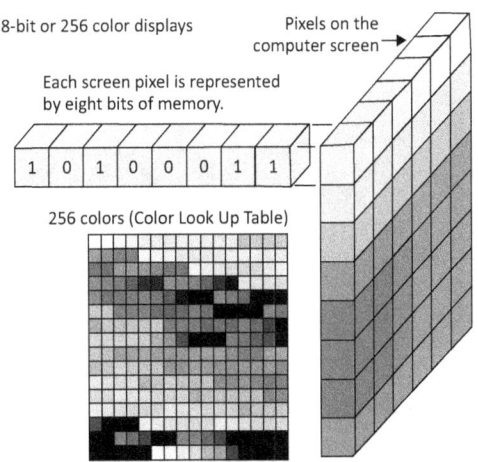

- **Image segmentation:** The system identifies and groups similar colors and segments the image, thus, distinguishing the foreground from the background. Techniques such as gradients are used to find edges between different objects.

Figure 6.5 How image segmentation works

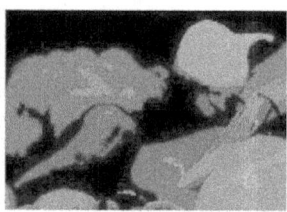

- **Corner (feature) detection:** After segmentation, the image is then analyzed for certain features, also known as corners. Algorithms search for lines that meet at an angle and cover a specific part of the image with one color shade. These features act as building blocks that help reveal more detailed information contained in the image.

Figure 6.6 Corner detection in image processing

- **Texture analysis:** Another important aspect of correctly identifying an image is determining the texture in the image. Differences in texture between regions make it easier for a model to categorize objects correctly.

| Figure 6.7 | Texture detection in image processing |

- **Prediction:** After implementing the above steps, the model makes a prediction by breaking down the image based on colors, corners, textures, etc. It then compares the result to the expected label (as defined by the training objective). In recent years, accuracy has improved greatly, but models can still make mistakes, especially with images containing multiple, overlapping, or ambiguous objects.

| Figure 6.8 | Identifying and labeling multiple objects in an image |

6.2.2 Image Classification

Image classification is a kind of biologically primary ability of the human visual perception system. It is an active task, and it plays a crucial role in the field of computer vision, which aims to automatically classify images into predefined classes. For decades, researchers have laid the groundwork to improve classification accuracy. Traditionally, classification models performed well only on small datasets. A major leap came in 2009 with the creation of the large-scale ImageNet dataset by Fei-Fei Li and her colleagues, coinciding with the rise of deep learning and its breakthrough results in vision.

This step has the ability to group entire images into predefined classes or categories (e.g., "cat," "dog," or "neither"). CNNs, specialized deep learning models for images, excel at learning complex hierarchies of features, enabling them to recognize intricate patterns and achieve highly accurate classifications. This foundational capability is the bedrock for various other computer vision applications.

Mainly, there are two types of image classification:

- **Single-label classification:** This is the most common type of image classification. In single-image classification, each image receives exactly one label from a set of mutually exclusive classes.

- **Multi-label classification:** This is a more complex classification. In this classification, an image can receive multiple labels simultaneously (e.g., medical images where a single X-ray may indicate more than one condition).

6.2.3 Object Tracking

Object tracking is a deep learning process where the algorithm tracks the movement of an object. In other words, it is the task of estimating or predicting the positions (and other attributes) of moving objects in a video. It is a fundamental technique in video analysis and often builds on object detection. The model first detects objects, draws bounding boxes around them, assigns each a unique ID, and then tracks those detections as they move through subsequent frames while storing relevant information. Although the idea sounds straightforward, reliable tracking is essential for many applications (e.g., surveillance, sports analytics, and autonomous driving) and can be challenging in the presence of occlusions, motion blur, or rapid appearance changes.

6.2.4 Semantic Segmentation

This phase takes object analysis to a whole new level by meticulously labeling each and every pixel within an image with a semantic category, e.g., color, contrast, location and other attributes. There are three related segmentation tasks:

- **Semantic segmentation:** Assigns a semantic class to every pixel in the image
- **Instance segmentation:** Identifies pixels and separates different instances of countable objects (e.g., person A vs. person B).
- **Panoptic segmentation:** Combines both; every pixel gets a semantic label, and object instances receive unique identifiers where applicable.

Imagine looking at a photo and not only identifying objects but also understanding the precise boundaries and categories of each pixel. This level of granularity opens up a world of advanced possibilities in robotics, medical imaging, autonomous driving, and more. Many state-of-the-art models rely on robust architectures such as FCNs, U-Nets, and DeepLab variants to achieve high accuracy.

6.3 Object Detection

Object detection is a task in computer vision that involves identifying and localizing objects of interest in images or video. The main purpose of object detection is to identify and locate one or more target objects within still images or video data. It comprehensively includes a variety of important techniques, such as image processing and pattern recognition. In essence, object detection combines image classification and object localization. It is a fundamental task in computer vision with a wide range of applications, including self-driving cars, robotics, and security systems. Now, let's simplify this concept further with the help of Figure 6.9.

Figure 6.9   **Example of object detection in images**

Instead of classifying which type of dog appears in these images, we first need to locate a dog: is it at the center, near the bottom, or on the left? Now, the next question that follows is: how can we do that? We can create a box around the dog and specify the X and Y coordinates of the box.

Figure 6.10   **Locating objects in images with bounding box coordinates**

In this context, the location of an object in an image can be represented by the coordinates of a bounding box, the box drawn around the object. This turns the task into an object localization (OL) problem: given a set of images, identify where the object appears in each image. OL means recognizing the existence of one or more objects in an image and marking the location with a bounding box. It consists of inputs and outputs. The inputs are the images that have objects that need to be located. The outputs consist of the bounding boxes that indicate the locations of objects.

Note that in the previous example we had a single class, but what if there are multiple classes? Here is an example.

Figure 6.11 **Multi-class object detection and localization**

In this image, we have to locate the objects, but note that not all the objects are dogs. Here we have a dog and a car. So we must not only locate the objects in the image but also classify the located object as a dog or a car. This makes it an object detection problem. In object detection, we have to classify the objects in the image and determine where they are located, whereas basic image classification has only one task: identifying what is in the image.

Broadly, object detection involves three tasks:

- Is there an object present in the image? (object presence)
- Where is the object located? (localization)
- What is the object? (classification)

6.3.1 Object Recognition

Object recognition includes image classification, object localization and object detection. It refers to classifying and locating objects in an image with a certain degree of accuracy, that is, how closely the object matches a recognized class.

Object recognition and object detection are related, but they differ in the way they operate. In deep learning, object detection is part of object recognition. Object detection focuses more on locating and classifying objects in an image, whereas object recognition mainly focuses on identifying objects.

Object recognition typically involves three processes:

- Classification
- Tagging
- Detection

Classification and tagging refer to labeling objects in an image with their particular classes or tags; in short, these two processes focus on identifying the contents of an image. Detection and segmentation refer to locating objects in an image (and, in the case of segmentation, delineating their precise shapes) after the objects have been identified.

Figure 6.12 Visual comparison of object recognition techniques

Semantic Segmentation	Classification + Localization	Object Detection	Instance Segmentation
GRASS, CAT, TREE, SKY	CAT	DOG, DOG, CAT	DOG, DOG, CAT
No objects, just pixels	Single Object	Multiple Object	

6.3.2 Stepwise Object Detection

The steps involved in object detection in computer vision can be summarized as follows:

- **Image preprocessing:** The first step in object detection is to preprocess the image to improve its quality and reduce noise. This involves tasks such as resizing, normalization, and filtering.

- **Feature extraction:** The next step is to extract features from the image that can be used to identify objects. This can be done using techniques such as Histogram of Oriented Gradients (HOG), Scale-Invariant Feature Transform (SIFT), and Convolutional Neural Networks (CNNs).

- **Object proposal generation:** Once features are extracted, the next step is to generate object proposals or candidate regions that are likely to contain objects of interest. This can be done using methods such as Selective Search or Edge Boxes.

- **Object classification:** The next step is to classify the object proposals as either containing an object of interest or not. This can be done using machine learning algorithms such as Support Vector Machines (SVMs) or CNNs.

- **Bounding box regression:** Once objects have been classified, the final step is to refine the bounding boxes around the objects of interest to accurately localize them in the image. This can be done using regression algorithms that adjust the coordinates of the bounding boxes based on the object's size, shape, and position.

6.3.3 Pattern Identification

Pattern recognition analyzes incoming data to identify patterns. The identification of regularities in data can then be used to make predictions, categorize information, and improve decision-making.

A typical image pattern-recognition task includes four steps: image acquisition, image preprocessing, feature extraction and classification. Pattern identification is the process of assigning an unknown pattern to one of several established categories based on features extracted from prior data. Just think, at the age of 5, most children can recognize digits and letters – small characters, large characters, handwritten, machine-printed, or rotated – often with ease. In many cases, humans are the best pattern recognizers, yet we do not fully understand how human pattern recognition works.

The rapidly growing volume of data makes manual interpretation impractical, driving the need for machines to identify patterns quickly and accurately. Automating the recognition of patterns and regularities in data has many applications today; examples are fingerprint analysis, face detection/verification. Object and pattern identification is a fundamental task in AI as it involves recognizing repeated shapes, colors, and other visual indicators to locate and classify objects within images. Popular deep-learning approaches include YOLO and R-CNN. In machine learning more broadly, algorithms are trained on datasets to recognize patterns; some methods rely on labeled data, while others do not.

Recognition and classification typically fall into two categories:

- **Supervised classification (descriptive):** identifies the input pattern as a member of a predefined class.
- **Unsupervised classification (exploratory):** assigns the input pattern to a hitherto undefined class based on similarity.

Thus, the recognition problem is usually posed as either a classification or categorization task. The classes are either defined by the system designer (supervised classification) or are learned based on the similarity of patterns (unsupervised classification). With this task framing in place, we can now look at classic feature-based methods, which extract distinctive, hand-crafted descriptors before classification.

Feature-Based Methods

- SIFT (Scale-Invariant Feature Transform): Helps in detecting the points of object in the image
- SURF (Speeded-Up Robust Features): A faster alternative to SIFT, commonly used for large applications

So far we've focused on recognizing patterns. Next, we turn to generative methods that create realistic images, most notably GANs.

6.4 Image Generation: Generative Adversarial Networks (GANs)

A GAN is a deep learning approach that enables computers to generate new, artificial data based on existing datasets. A GAN comprises two neural networks: a generator, which generates images, and a discriminator, which determines whether an image is real or fake. The discriminator is first trained on real data so that, when the generator produces synthetic images, it can learn to distinguish them from real ones. The generator tries to fool the discriminator, and the discriminator tries not to be fooled.

During training, the generator explores different parameter combinations and gradually improves its outputs until they look realistic enough that the discriminator can no longer reliably tell them apart from real data. When the discriminator judges an image as fake, it provides feedback that helps the generator adjust its parameters to better match the real data distribution. This adversarial process continues until an equilibrium is reached and the generator produces highly realistic results. Now that we know how GANs learn, let's look at where GANs are used in practice.

Applications of GANs include:

- Generating image, video, and text.
- Creating realistic images of people, animals, and objects.
- In healthcare, GANs have been shown to generate synthetic tumor images that can support diagnosis and treatment planning.
- Producing more realistic 3D content from 2D inputs by incorporating voxels, point clouds, or neural radiance fields.
- Enhancing image quality through super-resolution, i.e., upscaling low-resolution images to higher resolution.

Figure 6.13 | Architecture of a Generative Adversarial Network (GAN)

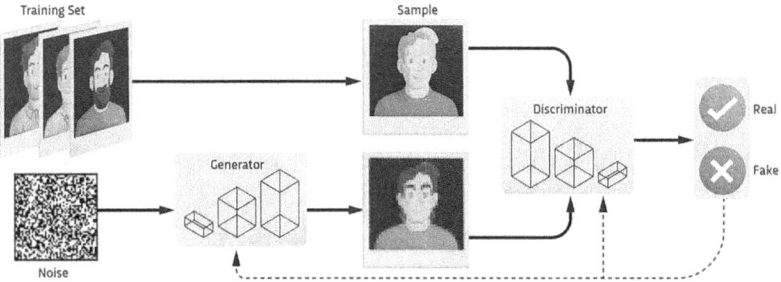

Let's look at the practical implementation of the same in a stepwise manner.

Step 1: Import Necessary Libraries

- TensorFlow is an open-source ML library that helps you build, train, and run deep learning models like GANs.

- Matplotlib is a Python library used to create static, interactive, and animated visualizations. In GAN projects, it is often used to display generated images.

```
import numpy as np
import tensorflow as tf
from tensorflow.keras import layers
import matplotlib.pyplot as plt
```

Step 2: Data Preparation

- The MNIST (Modified National Institute of Standards and Technology) dataset is a classic and widely used dataset which contains 70,000 grayscale images of handwritten digits ranging from 0 to 9.

- 60,000 images are used for training and 10,000 images are reserved for testing.

```
# Load and normalize MNIST dataset
(x_train, _), _ = tf.keras.datasets.mnist.load_data()
x_train = x_train / 127.5 - 1.0
x_train = np.expand_dims(x_train, axis=-1)

BUFFER_SIZE = 60000
BATCH_SIZE = 128
train_dataset = tf.data.Dataset.from_tensor_slices(x_train).shuffle(BUFFER_SIZE).batch(BATCH_SIZE)
```

Step 3: Model Definitions (Generator and Discriminator)

- Load and normalize the MNIST digits.
- Define the Generator (creates fake images) and the Discriminator (detects real/fake images).

```
# Define the Generator Model
def build_generator():
    model = tf.keras.Sequential([
        layers.Dense(7*7*256, use_bias=False, input_shape=(100,)),
        layers.BatchNormalization(),
        layers.LeakyReLU(),
        layers.Reshape((7, 7, 256)),
        layers.Conv2DTranspose(128, (5,5), strides=(1,1), padding='same', use_bias=False),
        layers.BatchNormalization(),
        layers.LeakyReLU(),
        layers.Conv2DTranspose(64, (5,5), strides=(2,2), padding='same', use_bias=False),
        layers.BatchNormalization(),
        layers.LeakyReLU(),
        layers.Conv2DTranspose(1, (5,5), strides=(2,2), padding='same', use_bias=False, activation='tanh')
    ])
    return model

# Define the Discriminator Model
def build_discriminator():
    model = tf.keras.Sequential([
        layers.Conv2D(64, (5,5), strides=(2,2), padding='same', input_shape=[28, 28, 1]),
        layers.LeakyReLU(),
        layers.Dropout(0.3),
        layers.Conv2D(128, (5,5), strides=(2,2), padding='same'),
        layers.LeakyReLU(),
        layers.Dropout(0.3),
        layers.Flatten(),
        layers.Dense(1)
    ])
    return model
```

Step 4: Loss Functions and Training Step

- Set up loss functions for both models.
- In each training step, the generator tries to fool the discriminator, while the discriminator tries to correctly identify fake images. Here, the loss function plays a crucial role.
- The generator is penalized when the discriminator successfully detects fake images.

```
# Loss function and optimizers
cross_entropy = tf.keras.losses.BinaryCrossentropy(from_logits=True)
generator = build_generator()
discriminator = build_discriminator()

generator_optimizer = tf.keras.optimizers.Adam(1e-4)
discriminator_optimizer = tf.keras.optimizers.Adam(1e-4)

# Single training step
@tf.function
def train_step(images):
    noise = tf.random.normal([BATCH_SIZE, 100])

    with tf.GradientTape() as gen_tape, tf.GradientTape() as disc_tape:
        generated_images = generator(noise, training=True)

        real_output = discriminator(images, training=True)
        fake_output = discriminator(generated_images, training=True)

        gen_loss = cross_entropy(tf.ones_like(fake_output), fake_output)
        disc_loss = cross_entropy(tf.ones_like(real_output), real_output) + \
                    cross_entropy(tf.zeros_like(fake_output), fake_output)

    gradients_of_generator = gen_tape.gradient(gen_loss, generator.trainable_variables)
    gradients_of_discriminator = disc_tape.gradient(disc_loss, discriminator.trainable_variables)

    generator_optimizer.apply_gradients(zip(gradients_of_generator, generator.trainable_variables))
    discriminator_optimizer.apply_gradients(zip(gradients_of_discriminator, discriminator.trainable_variables))
```

Step 5: Train the GAN and Generate Images

- Train the GAN using a training loop.
- After training, generate a fake digit image and displays it with Matplotlib.

```
import time

# Training loop
def train(dataset, epochs):
    for epoch in range(epochs):
        start = time.time()
        for image_batch in dataset:
            train_step(image_batch)
        print(f'Epoch {epoch+1} Completed in {time.time() - start:.2f}s')

# Train for 5 epochs
train(train_dataset, epochs=5)

# Generate and display a sample image
def generate_and_show():
    noise = tf.random.normal([1, 100])
    generated_image = generator(noise, training=False)
    plt.imshow(generated_image[0, :, :, 0], cmap='gray')
    plt.axis('off')
    plt.show()

generate_and_show()
```

The `generate_and_show()` function displays a grayscale image produced by the generator from random noise. As the training progresses through more epochs, the image quality gradually improves, eventually becoming nearly indistinguishable from real handwritten digits.

Points to Remember

- Increasing the number of epochs often makes generated images sharper and more realistic (almost like the original dataset). So, More Epochs → Better Learning → Clearer Images.

- As training continues through more epochs, the model gradually learns features and patterns of real digits/ images.

- Too many epochs can lead to overfitting.

- Use visual checks and/or loss curves to monitor performance and identify when the model is performing best.

6.5 Computer Vision Libraries

Computer vision libraries are essential for developers and researchers who need visual data in various applications. These libraries provide a collection of pre-built algorithms, functions, and tools that simplify the complex image and video analysis process.

OpenCV (Open Source Computer Vision Library): A library designed to operate in real-time for Computer Vision applications.

- Image and video processing.
- Object detection and tracking.
- Camera calibration and 3D reconstruction.

TensorFlow: A software library for ML & AI which helps in creating a model & easy to run in any environment

- Supports deep learning and machine learning models.
- TensorFlow Hub for reusable models.
- TensorFlow Lite for mobile and embedded devices.

Keras: A high-level neural networks API running on top of TensorFlow and Simplifies the creation and training of deep learning models

- Simplifies the creation and training of deep learning models.
- Modular and extensible.

Scikit-Image: A collection of algorithms for image processing in Python.

- Filtering, morphology, segmentation, and more.
- Integrates well with other scientific Python libraries.

Matlab: A high-level language and interactive environment for numerical computation, visualization, and programming.

- Image Processing Toolbox for computer vision applications.
- Simulink for model-based design.

6.6 Applications of Computer Vision

Computer vision aims to replicate the complexity of human vision. It can perform post-processing tasks with remarkable precision, often faster than any human. It relies heavily on machine learning and requires significant computational power.

Computer vision systems collect as much visual data as possible and then process that information so it can be applied to various tasks. This is what gives computer vision its flexibility. For example, it can count objects in an image or estimate their sizes with incredible accuracy. Think about the potential it holds in inventory management, quality control in manufacturing, or even in monitoring wildlife populations in conservation efforts. Computer vision has widespread applications across industries, including:

Healthcare

In recent years, AI and CV have shown excellent potential in improving disease detection, especially in identifying cancer-related tumors at an early stage. Computer vision systems assist doctors by highlighting suspicious regions in medical images, supporting more accurate and faster diagnosis and even prognosis prediction (for example, estimating how a disease might progress). CV can track the distribution and administration of medications, ensuring accuracy and safety. During the COVID-19 pandemic, governments used computer vision systems to monitor mask compliance in public spaces.

Autonomous Vehicles

Autonomous navigation in self-driving cars and drones depends heavily on AI and computer vision. These technologies detect and recognize objects while understanding their surroundings in detail. This is crucial for making quick decisions and safely moving through complex environments. For example:

- Object detection helps identify pedestrians, cyclists, and vehicles to avoid collisions.
- Lane detection and traffic sign recognition help the vehicle follow the rules of the road.
- Parking assistance and accident prevention systems use cameras and computer vision to support safe maneuvering in complex environments.

Agriculture

Today, farmers are leveraging computer vision to enhance agricultural productivity by using artificial intelligence models for sowing and harvesting purposes. Computer vision also supports weather-aware decision-making by analyzing field conditions alongside environmental data. Typical applications include:

- Drone-based crop monitoring to assess plant health and detect stress or disease early.

- Automatic spraying of pesticides and fertilizers with high precision, reducing waste and chemical overuse.

- Weed detection and removal using smart robotics.

- Yield tracking, grading, sorting, and classification of harvested produce to improve quality and reduce manual labor.

Security and Surveillance

With the widespread use of CCTV and smart cameras in public and private spaces, AI-driven video analytics has become a standard feature of surveillance systems. Computer vision can perform facial recognition for identity verification and access control, which is useful for security checkpoints and restricted areas. It can also assist in crime prevention and investigation by matching known profiles to captured footage (where legally permitted).

Another important use is anomaly detection: systems can automatically flag unusual or threatening activity in live video feeds, for example, unattended bags in public transport hubs or sudden crowd movements, enabling faster incident response and real-time threat analysis.

Retail and E-Commerce

Retail stores are already embracing computer vision solutions to monitor customer activity and improve both the customer experience and store operations. Some major applications include:

- Visual search for online shopping, where users can search for products using photos.
- Automated checkout systems using image recognition, such as Amazon Go stores.
- Inventory tracking using CV-powered shelf-scanning robots.
- Defect detection in production lines, ensuring high product quality.
- Automated sorting and packaging systems powered by robotic vision.

Entertainment and Media

Computer vision plays a huge role in how content is created, delivered, and personalized today. In films, it enables hyper-realistic CGI, face tracking for animation, and advanced video enhancement. Deepfake-style techniques (which can realistically alter faces and voices) are used both for special effects and, controversially, for synthetic media, raising important ethical questions.

In gaming and immersive media, computer vision supports AR/VR experiences that blend the physical and digital worlds, making gameplay feel more responsive and lifelike. In live sports broadcasting, AI-driven camera systems can automatically track players, choose intelligent camera angles, and generate instant replays without needing a human camera operator at every position.

On the content delivery side, streaming platforms use vision models to automatically tag and index video frames. This makes it easier to organize massive content libraries and power personalized recommendations for viewers.

However, every positive and growing technology has its own disadvantages and obstacles. The main limitations of CV are cost and accessibility, data privacy and ethical concerns, processing power and resource demands, data accuracy and quality, and integration complexity.

Computer vision is a groundbreaking technology with many exciting applications and what makes it even more unique is its adaptability. Through the power of machine learning and deep learning, these systems are evolving over time and making our life easier. That means they can become increasingly accurate and reliable as they process more data and gain more experience in the coming decades. This adaptability is what allows computer vision to continually push the boundaries of what's possible in various industries and applications.

In simple terms: computer vision helps computers "see" the world we live in, and then turns what it sees into insights and actions that can improve safety, quality, efficiency, and convenience. As of now, computer vision is expected to unlock the potential of many new and emerging technologies, supporting safer transportation, earlier disease detection, smarter cities, more sustainable farming, and richer interactive media. The end goal is not just automation for its own sake, but better quality of life for people.

 **Chapter Summary**

- Computer Vision (CV) enables machines to interpret and understand visual data using AI and deep learning, especially Convolutional Neural Networks (CNNs). It has evolved from basic image analysis to real-time applications like facial recognition, autonomous driving, and advanced medical imaging, with breakthroughs such as YOLO for instant object detection.

- CV workflows involve image capture, interpretation, and analysis to produce actionable insights. Essential tasks include feature extraction (colors, edges, textures), image classification (single/multi-label), object tracking, semantic segmentation (pixel-level labeling), and pattern identification using methods like SIFT, SURF, YOLO, and R-CNN.

- Object detection combines classification and localization, using bounding boxes to find and label multiple objects in an image. Steps include preprocessing, feature extraction, proposal generation, classification, and bounding box regression. Object recognition encompasses classification, tagging, detection, and segmentation.

- Generative Adversarial Networks use a generator (creates fake images) and discriminator (detects fakes) in a competitive loop until realistic images are produced. GANs have applications in image synthesis, upscaling, 3D reconstruction, and medical imaging simulations.

- CV powers innovations in healthcare (early diagnosis), autonomous vehicles, agriculture, surveillance, retail, manufacturing, and entertainment. Popular libraries include OpenCV, TensorFlow, Keras, Scikit-Image, and MATLAB. Despite its potential, challenges remain in cost, privacy, processing power, and data quality.

Quiz

1. **What was the major advancement in computer vision in the last two decades?**
   a. Introduction of analog cameras
   b. Creation of deep learning algorithms and CNNs
   c. Development of facial recognition
   d. Invention of smart home technologies

2. **What does YOLO stand for in computer vision?**
   a. You Only Learn Once
   b. Your Own Learning Operation
   c. You Only Look Once
   d. Your Object Location Optimizer

3. **Which of the following is a key component of computer vision?**
   a. Object tracking
   b. Memory allocation
   c. Database management
   d. Voice recognition

4. **In computer vision, how does a machine represent colors?**
   a. Through RGB spectrum analysis
   b. By specified HEX values
   c. Using binary color codes
   d. With natural language descriptions

5. **What is the purpose of image segmentation in computer vision?**
    a. To compress image files for storage
    b. To enhance color quality
    c. To distinguish foreground from background
    d. To encrypt visual data

6. **What are "corners" in the context of computer vision?**
    a. The physical edges of the image
    b. Features where lines meet at an angle
    c. Areas with the lowest pixel density
    d. Color anomalies in the image

7. **Which of the following is NOT one of the three main tasks in object detection?**
    a. Identify if there is an object present in the image
    b. Determine where the object is located
    c. Categorize what the object is
    d. Calculate the mass of the object

8. **What is semantic segmentation in computer vision?**
    a. Breaking an image into equal parts
    b. Labeling each pixel in an image with its respective category
    c. Removing unnecessary background elements
    d. Translating visual data into text

9. **What are Generative Adversarial Networks (GANs) used for?**
   a. To classify existing images
   b. To compress image files
   c. To generate new artificial data based on existing datasets
   d. To translate text to images

10. **In GANs, what is the role of the discriminator?**
    a. To generate fake images
    b. To determine whether images are real or fake
    c. To edit existing images
    d. To store image data

Answers

1 – b	2 – c	3 – a	4 – b	5 – c
6 – b	7 – d	8 – b	9 – c	10 – b

## CHAPTER 7

Generative AI

Key Learning Objectives

- Understand the core concepts and evolution of Generative AI (GenAI).
- Explore the rapidly evolving landscape of Generative AI across tools, models, and platforms.
- Learn the importance of Prompt Engineering in driving the outputs of Large Language Models (LLMs).
- Understand the fundamentals, capabilities, and architecture of Large Language Models (LLMs).
- Discover the real-world applications of GenAI in various domains.

7.1 Introduction to Generative AI

Have you ever stopped to wonder how your phone can finish your sentences before you even type them? Or how ChatGPT can write a poem that actually makes you feel something? You've probably come across those incredible AI-generated images that could easily hang in a museum, or maybe you've turned to AI when you were stuck debugging code late at night and couldn't find answers anywhere else like Stack Overflow. Sound like something you've experienced? Or if you're simply curious about the technology that's got everyone from tech CEOs to your grandmother talking, then you've come to the right place.

Let's break down what generative AI actually is and explore the mechanics behind how it operates, and more crucially, discover practical ways it can simplify your daily routine, boost your work efficiency, and add some enjoyment to the mix. We'll thoroughly examine prompt engineering – essentially learning how to communicate with these AI systems to achieve your desired results and navigate through the wide range of AI tools that are accessible today.

7.1.1 What Exactly is Generative AI, and Why Should You Care

What's so different about generative AI compared to the AI we've been talking about for ages?

Okay, so picture this. You know how you might teach a little kid to recognize animals? With traditional AI, it's like you sit there showing them picture after picture of cats and dogs - we're talking hundreds, maybe thousands of these photos. Eventually the kid gets really good at it. Show them a new picture and they'll tell you "cat" or "dog" pretty quickly. That's actually pretty impressive if you think about it. But Generative AI is a step further. Now imagine asking the same kid "Can you draw a cat from scratch?" - not copy one but to actually come up with their own version based on what they have learned. That's a much more creative task and that is exactly what Generative AI does. It just doesn't recognize patterns but it creates new content based on them. Whether it's writing a poem, composing music, generating an image, or a video snippet. Generative AI learns from massive data and then produces something original that didn't exist before.

| Figure 7.1 | Hierarchy of ML, deep learning, and generative AI |

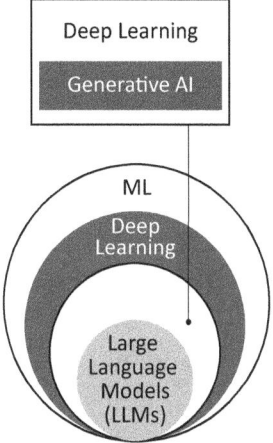

In more technical terms, generative AI is a type of artificial intelligence that can create entirely new content based on patterns it has learned from existing data. It's like having an incredibly well-read assistant who has absorbed millions of books, articles, images, and conversations, and can now create original content that feels authentic and human-like. This assistant doesn't just repeat what it has seen and it combines elements in new ways to create something that has never existed before.

But here's what really gets me excited about GenAI; this isn't just some cool party trick for making nice artwork or getting help with your English homework. Generative AI is actually flipping the script on how we deal with computers. Think about it - for years, we've been the ones doing all the work to communicate with our computers. You know the drill - clicking through a million different menus, filling out the forms where you have to put everything in exactly the right format, memorizing all these specific commands just to get anything done. But now? The tables are turning. These computers are finally starting to figure out how we actually talk and think. So instead of us having to bend over backwards to speak computer language, they're learning to speak ours.

Just imagine what this actually means for your day-to-day life. You know how you used to waste hours scrolling through endless stock photo websites trying to find that one perfect image for your work presentation? Now you can just tell the AI "I need a picture of a professional team meeting in a modern office" and boom - it creates exactly what you're looking for in just a few seconds. Or think about coding. Maybe you're not a programmer, but you have this idea for a simple app or tool that would make your life easier. Before, you'd either have to spend months learning to code or pay someone a lot of money to build it. Now you can literally just explain what you want the program to do, and the AI will write the code for you!

When it comes to writing, the impact of generative AI is especially clear. We've all been there - staring at a blank email trying to figure out how to word something important without sounding weird or unprofessional. These days, you can just jot down your main points and let AI give you three or four different ways to say it. Then you pick whichever one feels right. It's basically like having a really talented assistant who can do creative work, technical stuff, and writing - all just by talking to them normally.

Generative AI represents an advanced branch of artificial intelligence that creates fresh content after studying enormous datasets of existing material. Traditional AI systems are designed to classify or analyze information, but generative AI possesses the unique capability to produce entirely original text, images, audio, video, and code that has never been created before.

Consider this distinction: traditional AI might analyze thousands of feline photographs and develop the capability to accurately identify cats in new images. Generative AI, however, can synthesize an entirely original, photorealistic image of a cat that has never been photographed or drawn before.

Figure 7.2 Defining generative AI through the function $Y = f(X)$

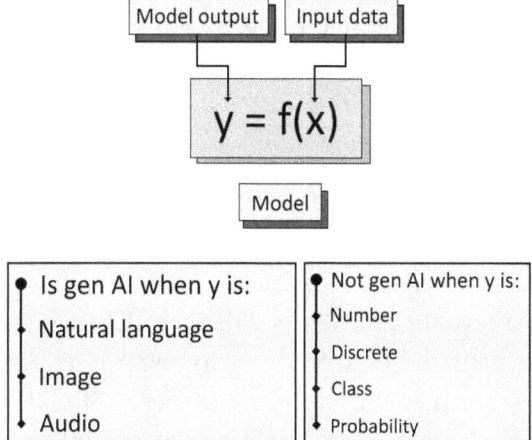

7.1.2 The Mathematical Foundation

We can visualize this concept mathematically as: $Y = f(X)$

Y: The model output (generated content)

f(): The function or model performing the transformation

X: The input data or prompt

The key differentiator? When Y is creative content (text, images, audio) rather than just a classification or number, we're in the realm of generative AI.

Figure 7.3 Process of creating new content using generative AI

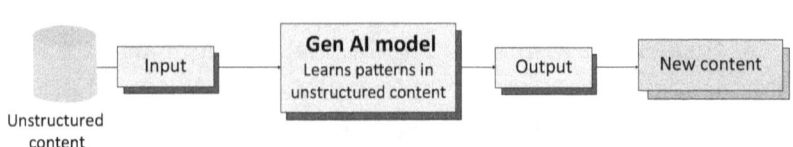

Generative AI learns in a similar way, but at a scale that's hard to fathom. A language model might read billions of web pages, books, articles, and conversations. A multi-modal model might analyze millions of photographs, paintings, and drawings. Through this massive exposure, the AI learns not just to recognize patterns but to understand the deep structures that underlie human creativity and communication.

For language models specifically, the training often involves playing a massive game of 'fill in the blank'. The AI reads a piece of text with some words hidden and tries to guess what the missing words are. When it guesses wrong, it adjusts its internal parameters – those billions of connections between its artificial neurons – to do better next time. Do this billions of times with billions of pieces of text, and you end up with a system that has an incredibly nuanced understanding of language.

But understanding is only half the equation. The real magic of generative AI is in the generation process, not by pulling pre-written responses from a database, but by predicting what comes next based on patterns it has learned from massive datasets. It's essentially a highly sophisticated text (or image/code/etc.) completion engine, using probability to decide the most likely next word, pixel, or token. This process isn't truly deterministic or creative in the human sense. It doesn't "think" or "understand" but it simulates those qualities by generating responses that look meaningful. And while that's often impressive, it can also lead to hallucinations: confident, fluent output that's factually incorrect or completely made up. That's the tradeoff. Generative AI can be incredibly useful, but its outputs need human judgment and verification.

7.2 Evolution of Generative AI

To truly appreciate where we are with generative AI today, we need to understand the remarkable journey of it through the last decade. There have been recent breakthroughs that transformed AI from an academic curiosity to a technology that's reshaping our world. Let me take you through the key moments and innovations that brought us to this extraordinary moment in technological history.

2014–2017: GANs & Transformer Revolution

During 2014, while most of us were obsessing over the Ice Bucket Challenge and debating whether that dress was blue and black or white and gold, a young researcher named Ian Goodfellow was having drinks with his colleagues at a bar in Montreal. The conversation turned to the limitations of existing AI systems, particularly their inability to generate new content. As the discussion progressed, Goodfellow had an idea that would revolutionize the field. What if, instead of training one neural network to create content, you trained two networks to compete against each other? This idea became known as Generative Adversarial Networks (GANs). Think of it like training a master art forger and a master art detective at the same time. The forger (called the generator) tries to create fake paintings that look real, while the detective (called the discriminator) tries to spot the fakes. As they compete, both get better – the forger creates increasingly convincing fakes, and the detective becomes better at spotting even the tiniest imperfections.

The beauty of this system is that it solved a fundamental problem in AI: how do you train a system to create something new when you can only show examples of what already exists? The adversarial approach provided the answer. The generator doesn't need to be explicitly told what makes a good image – it learns through the feedback of trying to fool the discriminator. Eventually, the generator becomes so good that even expert humans can't tell the difference between its creations and real images.

This breakthrough had immediate practical applications. Suddenly, AI could enhance low-resolution photos to high-resolution, transform sketches into photorealistic images, and even generate entirely new faces of people who never existed. The fashion industry began using GANs to design new clothing, architects used them to explore building designs, and researchers used them to augment limited datasets for training other AI systems.

Around the same time, another crucial innovation was happening with encoder-decoder systems. These architectures work like universal translators, but not just for languages. They can take one type of content (the input) and transform it into another type (the output). The encoder compresses the input into a dense representation that captures its core meaning, and the decoder reconstructs that into a new form, whether it's a translation, a caption, or even a visual representation.

If 2014 was about competition, 2017 was about attention – literally. A team of researchers at Google published a paper with the modest title "Attention Is All You Need," which turned out to be one of the most important papers in the history of AI. They introduced something called the Transformer architecture, and if GANs were like inventing the wheel, Transformers were like inventing the combustion engine.

To understand why Transformers were so revolutionary, imagine you're trying to understand a long, complex sentence. Traditional AI systems would read it word by word, sequentially, like reading through a straw. By the time they got to the end of the sentence, they might have forgotten what the beginning was about. It's like trying to understand a movie by watching it one frame at a time – you lose the bigger picture.

Transformers changed this completely. They introduced the concept of "self-attention," which allows the model to look at the entire sentence at once and understand how each word relates to every other word. It's like being able to see the whole page of a book at once, understanding not just the individual words but how they all connect to create meaning.

Figure 7.4 Workflow of a transformer model in NLP

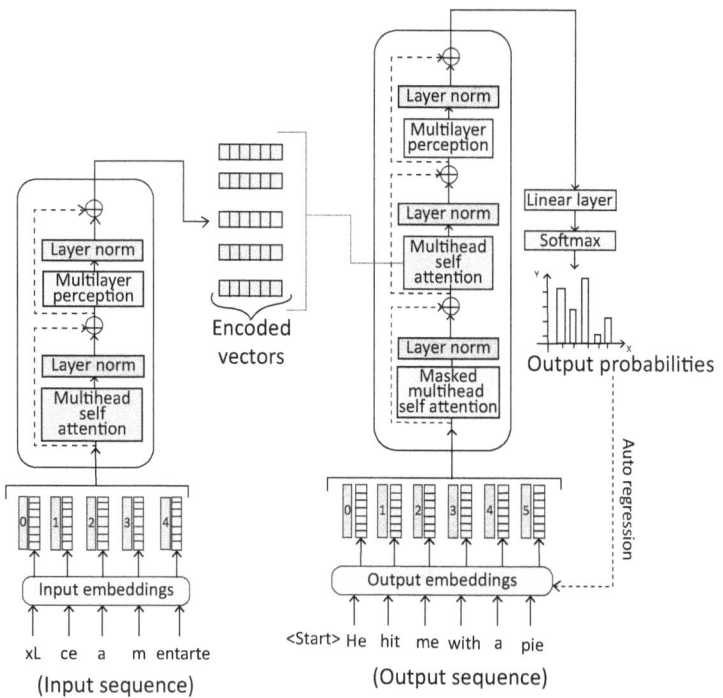

Figure 7.5 Live demonstration of self-attention processing our example sentence

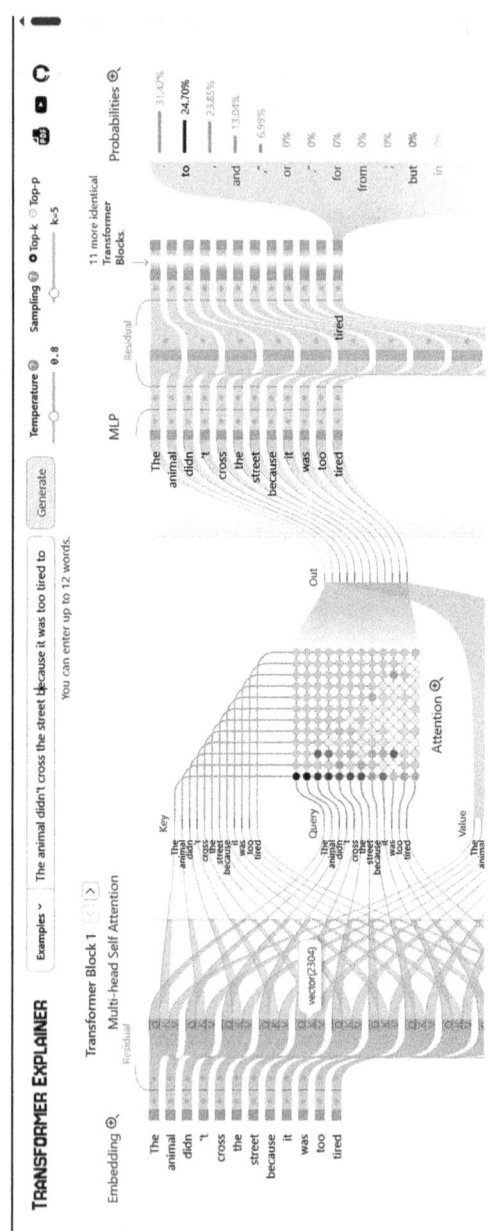

Source: Transformer Explainer visualization tool.

Let me give you a concrete example. Consider the sentence:

"The animal didn't cross the street because it was too tired."

What does "it" refer to – the animal or the street? A human instantly knows "it" refers to the animal (streets don't get tired), but for an AI, this requires understanding the relationship between all the words in the sentence. The attention mechanism allows the AI to connect "it" with "animal" and "tired" to correctly interpret the meaning.

Here's a visualization of how self-attention actually works in practice. When the model processes the phrase 'The animal didn't cross the street because it was too tired', it calculates attention scores between every word.

The shaded lines show attention weights between words, revealing how the model understands that "it" refers to "animal" (not "street") by examining all word relationships simultaneously. The model correctly predicts "to" as the most likely continuation.

Notice how the attention mechanism creates connections between related words across the entire sentence. The word 'it' shows strong attention patterns to 'animal' and 'tired,' helping the model understand the correct reference. This is fundamentally different from older models that would process words sequentially and might lose track of these long-distance relationships.

But the real magic of Transformers wasn't just in their ability to understand – it was in their ability to scale. Previous AI architectures would become impossibly slow and complex as you made them bigger. Adding more parameters (think of these as the AI's capacity to learn) meant exponentially longer training times and diminishing returns. Transformers, with their parallel processing abilities, could be scaled up to enormous sizes while still remaining (relatively) efficient to train.

2018–2020: The Large Language Model Era

With the Transformer architecture in place, the race was on to see just how powerful these systems could become, with different research labs competing to build bigger and better models. OpenAI fired the first shot with GPT (Generative Pre-trained Transformer) in 2018. The idea was beautifully simple yet completely revolutionary. Take the Transformer architecture, make it really big (117 million parameters), and train it on a huge chunk of the internet. The "pre-trained" part was crucial, instead of training a new model for each specific task, you could train one general model on vast amounts of text and then fine-tune it for specific applications. The results were impressive. GPT could complete sentences, answer questions, and even write short passages that were coherent and contextually appropriate. But this was just the beginning. In 2019, OpenAI released GPT-2 with 1.5 billion parameters (10X larger than its predecessor). The improvement wasn't just quantitative but was qualitative. GPT-2 could write entire essays, maintain consistency across long passages, and even demonstrate primitive reasoning abilities.

The research community was stunned. GPT-2 was so capable that OpenAI initially hesitated to release the full model, concerned about potential misuse. They worried about automated disinformation campaigns, spam that was indistinguishable from human writing, and other malicious applications. This sparked important conversations about AI safety and responsible disclosure that continue today.

Then came 2020 and GPT-3, with 175 billion parameters. To put this in perspective, if GPT-1 was a bicycle and GPT-2 was a car, GPT-3 was a rocket ship. The increase in capability wasn't linear – it was exponential. GPT-3 could do things that seemed impossible just a few years earlier. It could write in different styles, solve complex problems, translate between languages it had never been explicitly trained on, and even write code based on natural language descriptions.

But perhaps the most remarkable thing about GPT-3 was its ability to learn from just a few examples – a capability called "few-shot learning." Show it a couple of examples of a new task – like converting movie descriptions into emoji sequences or writing haikus about programming languages – and it could generalize and perform that task on new inputs. This meant that GPT-3 wasn't just a language model; it was a general-purpose AI system that could be adapted to almost any task involving language.

2022–2023: The ChatGPT Bubble

Everything changed on November 30, 2022. That's the day OpenAI released ChatGPT to the public, and the world would never be the same. Within five days, it had a million users. Within two months, it had 100 million. It was the fastest-growing consumer application in history, surpassing even TikTok and Instagram in adoption speed. But ChatGPT wasn't just GPT-3 with a chat interface slapped on top. It represented a fundamental shift in how AI systems were trained and deployed. After the initial language model training, ChatGPT went through a process called Reinforcement Learning from Human Feedback (RLHF). Here's how it worked: human trainers would have conversations with the AI, rank its responses, and provide feedback on what kinds of answers were helpful, harmless, and honest.

This training process transformed ChatGPT from a powerful but sometimes unpredictable language model into a helpful assistant. It learned to admit when it didn't know something instead of making up plausible-sounding nonsense. It learned to refuse harmful requests while explaining why. It learned to engage in multi-turn conversations while maintaining context and consistency. It was like the difference between a brilliant but eccentric professor who might go off on tangents and a thoughtful teaching assistant who focuses on helping you understand. The impact was immediate and profound. Suddenly, everyone from students writing essays to CEOs drafting strategies had access to an AI assistant that could help with virtually any text-based task. Teachers used it to create lesson plans, programmers used it to debug code, writers used it to overcome writer's block, and millions of people used it for everything from planning vacations to understanding complex topics.

2024–2025: The Multimodal Era and Specialized Intelligence

We're in what I call the multimodal era. The latest AI systems don't just understand and generate text but they seamlessly work with images, audio, video, and even code. The latest GPT models can look at a hand-drawn sketch of a website and write the HTML and CSS to build it. Claude can read a complex technical diagram and explain it in simple terms your grandmother would understand. Google's Gemini can watch a video and summarize its content, answer questions about what happened, and even generate a script for a similar video.

We're also seeing an explosion of specialized models. While large general-purpose models continue to improve, there's a growing ecosystem of smaller, focused models that excel at specific tasks. There are models optimized specifically for code generation that understand programming languages better than general models. There are models trained on scientific literature that can help researchers explore hypotheses and find connections between papers. There are models focused on creative writing that can maintain narrative consistency across entire novels. The competition between major AI labs – OpenAI,

Anthropic, Google, Meta, and others has driven rapid innovation. Each new model release seems to push the boundaries of what's possible. We're seeing improvements not just in raw capability but in efficiency, with models becoming smaller and faster while maintaining or even improving their performance. Some models can now run on personal devices, bringing powerful AI capabilities to your laptop or even your phone.

7.3 The Current Generative AI Landscape

Now that we understand how we got here, let's get practical. What tools are actually available to you right now? The landscape is rich and varied, with options for every need, budget, and skill level. Let me walk you through the major players and help you understand which tool might be right for your specific needs. This section provides a high-level overview of key tools and platforms in the Generative AI landscape. A more technical exploration of how these models function internally will be covered in Section 7.5 on Large Language Models.

7.3.1 OpenAI's ChatGPT

ChatGPT remains the most recognized name in AI, and for good reason. It's like the iPhone of the AI world, not always the most advanced in every single category, but consistently reliable, user-friendly, and versatile enough to handle almost anything you throw at it.

OpenAI has significantly evolved its model lineup in 2025. The current flagship models accessible through ChatGPT include:

GPT-4o (Omni): This is now the default model for many ChatGPT users (including limited access for free users, with higher limits for Plus subscribers). It's a multimodal model, processing and generating content seamlessly across text, audio, and images.

OpenAI o3 (and o3-pro): Positioned as OpenAI's "logic powerhouse," o3 excels in structured reasoning, complex problem-solving, science, planning, and mathematics. It's designed to "think" longer and evaluate alternatives before providing an answer, making it invaluable for tasks requiring deep analysis and reliability. The 'o3-pro' version, available to Pro users, offers even more computational power and higher accuracy for the most complex queries.

GPT-4.1 (and 4.1-mini): These models, particularly GPT-4.1, offer significant upgrades in coding, instruction following, and long-context comprehension. They are designed for advanced programming, working with large datasets, and technical projects. GPT-4.1 mini provides similar performance with lower latency and cost, making it efficient for high-volume technical applications.

o4-mini & o4-mini-high: Optimized for speed and cost-efficiency, these models excel in STEM reasoning, coding, and technical analysis, especially when budget is a concern. While fast, some sources suggest they can be less reliable for general tasks compared to GPT-4o or o3.

The free tier now typically grants access to GPT-4o (with limitations) and GPT-4.1 mini (unlimited), which are remarkably capable for everyday tasks. Need help writing an email? It's got you covered. Want to brainstorm ideas? No problem. The paid version of ChatGPT Plus subscription unlocks access to a wider range of these advanced models like GPT-4o, o3, o4-mini, o4-mini-high, GPT-4.1, GPT-4.1-mini.

GPT-5 (default model): GPT-5 is OpenAI's flagship model and powers the latest versions of ChatGPT for most users. It is multimodal (text, images, and other media) and focuses on much stronger reasoning, more accurate answers, and better coding abilities than GPT-4o or o3. It can automatically decide when to respond quickly and when to "think" longer and more deeply, making it feel more like interacting with a true subject-matter expert.

GPT-5.1 (Instant and Thinking): GPT-5.1 is an upgraded version of GPT-5 that OpenAI released later in 2025, with a strong focus on reliability and user experience. It comes in two coordinated variants: GPT-5.1 Instant, which is tuned for fast, conversational everyday use, and GPT-5.1 Thinking, which allocates more computation to harder problems and more complex analysis. Together, they provide warmer, more natural conversations, better instruction-following, fewer hallucinations, and improved control over tone and style, while still handling long context and multimodal inputs.

Sora: Beyond text and image, OpenAI also offers its groundbreaking text-to-video model. It was released for ChatGPT Plus and Pro users back in December 2024, Sora can generate realistic and imaginative video clips up to a minute long from text based prompts. It works well in creating complex scenes with multiple characters and specific types of motion while maintaining visual quality and adherence to the user's prompt. This capability dramatically expands the creative potential directly within the OpenAI ecosystem for users looking to produce dynamic visual content.

What makes ChatGPT special is its versatility and consistency. I've seen people use it for everything from planning their wedding (complete with vendor comparisons and budget breakdowns) to debugging complex code that had stumped them for hours. It's equally comfortable helping a fifth-grader with homework or assisting a PhD candidate with research. The interface is clean and simple – just a chat window where you type your questions or requests – making it accessible to anyone regardless of technical expertise. For the first time in history, AI felt like it had a face — something that everyday people could see, talk to, and actually use at scale!

7.3.2 Google's Gemini

Gemini is one of the strong competitors to OpenAI's ChatGPT. Where ChatGPT leans conversational, Gemini leans connected. It integrates deeply into the Google ecosystem, so if your life is in Gmail, Docs, Sheets, and Drive, Gemini acts like a supercharged assistant who already knows your workflow & it is available on every screen of Google's applications.

Its standout feature? Real-time web access. Ask it about breaking news or research papers from last week, and it'll pull live data — with sources. Planning travel, comparing trends, summarizing reports, Gemini is fast becoming the go-to for info-heavy tasks.

Gemini 3 Pro: This is Google's most advanced model, excelling at highly complex tasks with enhanced reasoning, advanced coding capabilities, and native multimodal support (up to 1 million tokens of context). It's ideal for exploring vast datasets.

Gemini 3 Flash & Flash-Lite: These models are optimized for speed. Flash-Lite is a newer, lowest-latency Flash variant in the Gemini 3 family, making it perfect for high-throughput tasks such as classification or summarization. They offer "thinking" controls (a configurable "reasoning budget") to improve efficiency.

Veo 3.1: Google has also released its most advanced video-generation model (unveiled at Google I/O 2025 in May, with Veo 3.1 upgrade in October 2025). It is now widely available for Google AI Pro subscribers (with limited daily generations, e.g., 3-5 videos) and offers full access via the Ultra tier.

Google's flagship text-to-video model can generate high-quality 1080p clips up to 8 seconds long, with synchronized native audio (including dialogue and sound effects). It also offers strong cinematic controls, accurate real-world physics, lip-syncing, and consistent characters and objects across shots.

7.3.3 Anthropic's Claude

Claude, created by Anthropic, is the AI that thinks before it speaks. It's known for structured responses, ethical guardrails, and a massive context window (up to 200K tokens). That means it can read and respond to entire books, legal documents, or sprawling research papers.

Claude Opus 4.5: As of late 2025, Claude Opus 4.5 is Anthropic's leading model (released in November 2025). It's renowned for best-in-class coding, agentic workflows (e.g., multi-hour autonomous tasks), enterprise use cases such as spreadsheets and financial analysis, and superior reasoning for complex computer-use tasks.

Claude Sonnet 4.5 (lighter model): Released in September 2025, Sonnet 4.5 offers improved performance over prior Sonnet versions and balances speed, cost, and capability. It's well suited for scaled deployments, such as rapid iteration or use as sub-agents.

Where Claude shines is when you want your AI to explain itself — to show its steps, weigh its uncertainties, or walk you through complex reasoning. It's slower, but often smarter. For legal, academic, or product design use cases, Claude feels more like a collaborator than a chatbot.

7.3.4 Meta's Llama

Meta's Llama or Meta.ai models are changing the game for those who want control. While not available directly through a chat interface, Llama's open-source availability means developers can run powerful models locally or fine-tune them for specialized tasks.

Llama 3: Released earlier in 2025, this model delivered impressive performance that rivals GPT-4 and because it's free to modify, there's been an explosion of community-built applications. If you're concerned about data privacy or want full-stack customization, Llama-based solutions are worth exploring.

Llama 4: Launched in April 2025, Llama 4 is designed to be natively multimodal, meaning they can handle both text and images effectively. Thousands of developers and companies have built applications on top of Llama, creating specialized tools for everything from medical diagnosis to legal research.

7.3.5 DeepSeek's R1

DeepSeek's R1 is the latest entrant, and it has made waves in 2025 for its exceptional ability to handle multi-step reasoning, complex programming tasks, and structured thinking with extremely low latency. Built as a reinforcement-tuned assistant agent, R1 isn't just about answering questions; it's designed to plan, execute, and reflect like a tireless junior engineer or analyst.

DeepSeek-R1-0528: Released on May 28, 2025, this version boasts improved benchmark performance, enhanced front-end capabilities, and reduced hallucinations. It supports JSON output and function calling, and its weights are open-source.

What sets R1 apart is its reasoning capabilities - how it breaks down tasks into smaller components, solves them methodically, and even evaluates the quality of its own responses. It's particularly strong at writing and debugging code, handling long documents, and offering self-reflective explanations on how it arrived at a solution. For developers and technical users, this model feels like working alongside a logical, patient collaborator.

Beyond the top five, there's a thriving ecosystem of specialized AI tools, each excellent at specific tasks. For example, Perplexity has reimagined web search by combining it with AI. Instead of giving you a list of links, it provides direct answers to your questions with citations to sources. It's like having a research assistant who instantly reads through search results and synthesizes them into a coherent answer. Midjourney and Stable Diffusion lead the pack in image generation. Midjourney (currently v7), accessible primarily through Discord but with a growing web platform, has become famous for its artistic, often dreamlike images. Stable Diffusion, being open-source, offers more control and customization options. Similarly, Google's Imagen 3 (available through Gemini and ImageFX) provides powerful capabilities for realistic and detailed image creation, including text integration. Lastly, GitHub Copilot and Cursor AI has revolutionized programming by suggesting code completions, writing entire functions based on comments, and helping debug issues. It's trained on millions of public code repositories, so it understands not just syntax but coding patterns and best practices.

With so many options, which one to choose? Here's my practical advice based on extensive experience:

- If you're just starting out, begin with ChatGPT or Claude's free tier. They're very user-friendly, and will help you understand what AI can do for you.
- If you need real-time information frequently, Gemini or Perplexity are your best bets. Their real-time search capabilities ensure you're always working with the latest data.

- If you're working with sensitive data, consider Claude for its thoughtful approach to privacy or explore Llama-based solutions that you can run locally.

- If you're a developer, try the R1, Cursor AI or GitHub Copilot. Also explore the APIs offered by OpenAI, Anthropic, and others to integrate AI into your applications.

- If you're in a creative field, explore Midjourney or Stable Diffusion for artistic images and ChatGPT for creative writing.

Remember, these tools aren't mutually exclusive. Many professionals use multiple AI tools, choosing the best one for each specific task. The free tiers are generous enough that you can experiment without financial commitment.

7.4 Prompt Engineering

Now we come to one of the most crucial skills in the AI age - prompt engineering. If generative AI is a powerful engine, prompt engineering is knowing how to drive it. It's the difference between getting mediocre, generic responses and receiving exactly what you need. Let me share everything I've learned about crafting effective prompts through countless hours of experimentation and real-world application.

7.4.1 Understanding the Fundamentals of Prompt Engineering

At its core, prompt engineering is about clear, strategic communication. But unlike human communication, where we rely on shared context, body language, tone of voice, and the ability to clarify misunderstandings in real-time, AI communication requires us to be more explicit and structured. Think of it this way - when you talk to a colleague about a project, they know your working style, the company culture, past projects you've done together, and countless other contextual details. The AI knows none of this unless you tell it. This isn't a limitation – it's actually a feature. It means the AI can adapt to any context you provide, becoming an expert in your specific situation at that moment.

7.4.2 Prompt Structure

Every effective prompt has several key components. You don't always need all of them, but understanding each helps you craft better requests:

Figure 7.6 Key elements for crafting effective prompts

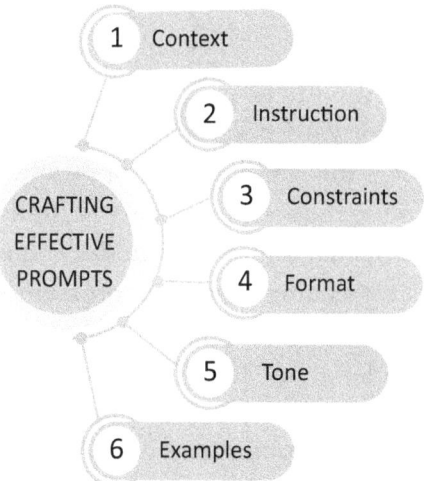

- **Context** sets the stage. "I'm a high school biology teacher preparing a lesson on photosynthesis for 10th graders who struggle with science concepts."
- **Instruction** provides the specific task. "Create a simple analogy that explains how photosynthesis works."

- **Constraints** set boundaries. "Keep it under 200 words and avoid technical jargon."

- **Format** specifies structure. "Present it as a story about a hungry plant."

- **Tone** defines style. "Make it engaging and slightly humorous, like Bill Nye would explain it."

- **Examples** show rather than tell. "Similar to how you might explain digestion by comparing it to a factory processing raw materials."

7.4.3 Prompting Techniques

Let me walk you through the major prompting techniques with practical examples:

Zero-Shot Prompting: Direct and Simple

Zero-shot prompting is a technique in which you ask for what you want without providing examples. It works well for straightforward tasks where the AI likely has good training data. It is the simplest type of prompt. It provides no examples to the model, just the instructions. In zero-shot, we provide no labeled data to the model and expect the model to work on a completely new problem. In the context of prompt engineering, zero-shot learning can be used to generate natural language text without the need for explicit programming or pre-defined templates. Zero-shot prompts are typically broader and more open ended. They provide a general theme or concept without specifying any particular details or constraints.

Basic: "Write a thank you email."

Better: "Write a professional thank you email to a client who just renewed their annual contract. Express genuine appreciation, mention our continued partnership, and end with looking forward to another successful year. Keep it warm but professional, around 150 words."

The second version works better because it provides context, specific elements to include, tone guidance, and length constraints.

One-Shot Prompting: Learning by Example

One-shot prompting shows the model one clear, descriptive example of what you'd like it to imitate. One-shot prompting is used to generate natural language text with a limited amount of input data such as a single example or template. They are more specific and often provide more detailed instructions or constraints. Sometimes showing is more effective than telling. One-shot prompting provides a single example:

"Convert book titles to emoji sequences:

'The Hunger Games' → 🏹📦🔥💀

Now convert: 'Harry Potter and the Sorcerer's Stone' →"

The AI understands from your example that it should use 3-4 emojis that capture the essence of the story.

Few-Shot Prompting: Pattern Recognition

A Few-shot prompting model is given a few examples, in order to quickly adapt to new examples of previously seen objects. These prompts provide a bit more direction or specificity compared to one-shot prompts They are much more specific to the context. For more complex tasks, multiple examples help establish patterns:

"Classify customer feedback:

'The app crashes every time I try to upload photos' → Bug Report

'I love the new dark mode feature!' → Positive Feedback

'Could you add the ability to schedule posts?' → Feature Request

'The latest update broke the export function' → Bug Report

'Great customer service experience today' → Positive Feedback

Now classify: 'The search function returns irrelevant results' →"

Chain-of-Thought Prompting: Show Your Work

Chain-of-thought prompting is a method that encourages the model to explain its reasoning. In chain-of-thought prompting, the input question is followed by a series of intermediate natural language reasoning steps that lead to the final answer. Think of this as breaking down a complicated task into bite-sized, logical chunks. Usually it is combined with one shot to generate effective results. For complex reasoning, ask the AI to think step-by-step:

"A company has 120 employees. 40% work in sales, 25% in engineering, 20% in marketing, and the rest in operations. If the company plans to increase engineering by 50% and reduce sales by 10%, how many employees will be in each department? Let's solve this step by step."

This approach dramatically improves accuracy for mathematical and logical problems. It also can help reduce hallucinations.

Point to Remember

Hallucinations in AI refer to instances where a model generates information that is factually incorrect or not grounded in the input data.

Role-Based Prompting: Expertise on Demand

Role prompting is a method where the AI model is designated a specific role such as programmer, a lawyer, a Devops engineer etc. The underlying principle is that providing the AI with some contextual information through a role can enhance its comprehension of the query, thereby often leading to more effective responses. Assigning a specific role helps frame responses appropriately:

"You are an experienced venture capitalist evaluating startups. A founder pitches: 'We're building an AI-powered personal shopping assistant that learns user preferences and suggests outfits.'

Provide your analysis considering:

- Market opportunity

- Competitive landscape

- Potential challenges

- Investment recommendation"

Iterative Prompting: Refining to Perfection

Iterative prompt engineering is a systematic approach to crafting prompts and refining them through successive iterations. The output of the e initial prompt serves as the starting point for iterative improvement/continuation. In iterative prompting, the model's response is analyzed for accuracy and relevance to the objective to identify key areas where it falls short. The follow-up iterative prompt is meant to address the identified issues or to continue generating the response. The iteration can be repeated if necessary. Ensure the prompt holds contextual information via an iterative process. Real mastery comes from understanding that prompting is often iterative:

Attempt 1: "Write about coffee."

Attempt 2: "Write a 300-word blog post about the health benefits of coffee for busy professionals."

Attempt 3: "Write a 300-word blog post about the health benefits of coffee for busy professionals. Include 3 specific benefits backed by research, address common concerns about caffeine, and end with practical tips for healthy coffee consumption. Use an informative but conversational tone."

This principle of refinement applies to all types of generative AI, not just text. Here's a visual example showing how better prompts lead to better results:

Figure 7.7 **The difference between vague and specific prompts in AI image generation**

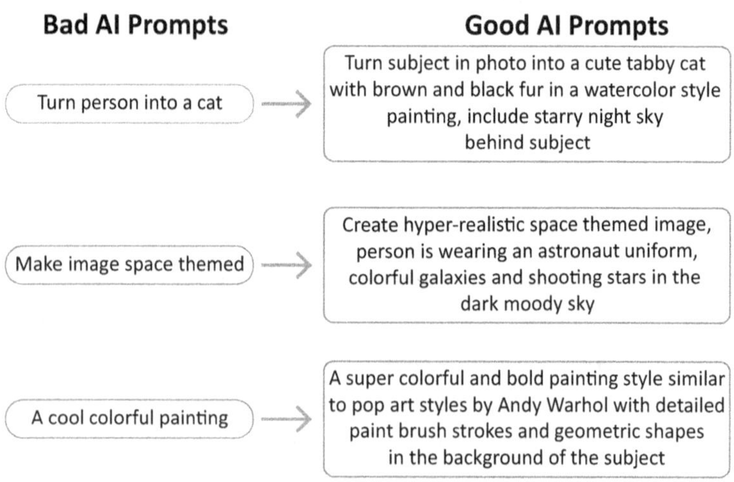

Bad AI Prompts		Good AI Prompts
Turn person into a cat	→	Turn subject in photo into a cute tabby cat with brown and black fur in a watercolor style painting, include starry night sky behind subject
Make image space themed	→	Create hyper-realistic space themed image, person is wearing an astronaut uniform, colorful galaxies and shooting stars in the dark moody sky
A cool colorful painting	→	A super colorful and bold painting style similar to pop art styles by Andy Warhol with detailed paint brush strokes and geometric shapes in the background of the subject

Notice how the "good" prompts include specific details about style, colors, composition, and artistic references, resulting in more controlled and desirable outputs. The same principle applies to all generative AI interactions.Whether you're generating text, images, code, or any other content, the pattern is clear: specificity and iteration lead to success. The 'bad' prompts leave too much to chance, while the 'good' prompts guide the AI toward exactly what you envision. This is why mastering prompt engineering is so crucial – it's the difference between hoping for good results and consistently achieving them.

7.4.4 Common Pitfalls and How to Avoid Them

Even experienced users make these mistakes:

- **Being too vague:** Don't ask broad questions like "Write something about marketing." Instead, be specific: "Write a 500-word guide on content marketing strategies for B2B SaaS startups, focusing on LinkedIn and email campaigns."

- **Information overload:** Don't dump entire documents. Summarize key points relevant to your request.

- **Assuming knowledge:** The AI doesn't know your company, preferences, or context unless you provide it.

- **Ignoring tone:** The same information can be delivered many ways. Always specify if you want formal, casual, technical, or any other specific tone.

- **Not iterating:** Your first prompt rarely produces perfect results. Plan to refine based on initial output.

7.5 Large Language Models (LLMs)

Large Language Models (LLMs) are the foundation of modern generative AI. Understanding how they work, even at a basic level, helps you use them more effectively. This section breaks down these complex systems into concepts anyone can understand.

7.5.1 What Makes a Language Model "Large"?

The "large" in Large Language Models refers to their massive scale – billions of parameters (adjustable weights), trained on enormous datasets, requiring vast computational resources. But size alone doesn't tell the whole story. These models achieve something remarkable: they develop emergent capabilities that smaller models simply don't have.

Large Language Models are foundational machine learning models that use deep learning algorithms to process and understand natural language. Trained on massive text datasets, they can understand instructions, follow context, and produce useful responses across a wide range of tasks.

Figure 7.8 Inputs and outputs in an LLM workflow

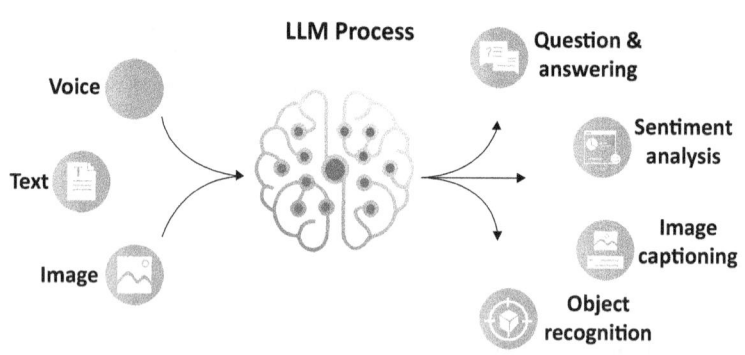

Think of it like this - a small model might learn that "cat" often appears near "meow" and "fur." A larger model learns not just word associations but concepts, relationships, context, and even abstract reasoning. It understands that cats are pets, mammals, independent creatures, subjects of internet memes, and symbols in literature – all from analyzing patterns in text. The combination of Transformers, massive data, and sophisticated training techniques created LLMs that can perform general-purpose reasoning and task execution, not just autocomplete sentences.

7.5.2 Small Language Models vs. Large Language Models

When discussing generative AI, conversations often focus on massive models like GPT-4 with its trillion parameters. However, there's a growing movement toward Small Language Models (SLMs) that proves bigger isn't always better. Think of it like choosing between a Swiss Army knife and a specialized tool – each has its place depending on your needs. Small Language Models typically have fewer than 10 billion parameters, often ranging from just a few million to a few billion. While GPT-3 has 175 billion parameters, models like Microsoft's Phi-2 achieve remarkable performance with just 2.7 billion parameters – that's less than 2% of GPT-3's size. SLMs like Mistral 7B and Phi-2 follow this streamlined approach to achieve efficiency with fewer than 10 billion parameters.

Figure 7.9 SLM development process showing the five key stages

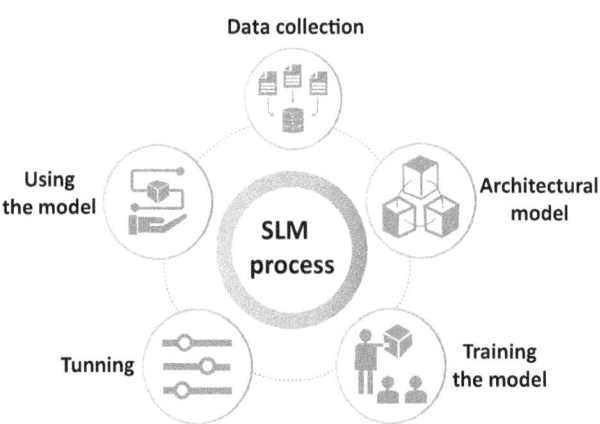

SLMs are designed with efficiency in mind. They can run on consumer hardware, process requests locally for privacy, and respond faster than their larger counterparts. This makes them ideal for edge computing, mobile applications, and scenarios where sending data to the cloud isn't practical or desirable.

7.5.3 Key Differences Between LLMs and SLMs

While these models solve many of the same problems (language understanding, reasoning, generation), they do so with very different tradeoffs in scale, cost, and deployment. The following table highlights the most important differences.

Table 7.1 Differences between LLMs and SLMs

Large Language Models	Small Language Models
10 billion to over 1 trillion parameters	Under 10 billion parameters (often 1-7 billion)
Require high-end GPUs (multiple A100s or H100s)	Run on consumer GPUs or even CPUs
Need 10s to 100s of GB of memory	Need 4-16 GB of memory
Must run in cloud environments	Can be deployed locally on devices
High energy consumption	Minimal energy consumption

7.5.4 Capabilities and Use Cases

LLMs excel at complex reasoning, creative writing, and handling diverse queries across all domains. They're ideal for research, analysis, and general-purpose AI assistants. SLMs, while more limited in scope, shine in specialized tasks, real-time processing, and privacy-sensitive applications. They often match or exceed LLMs in their specific domains while using a fraction of the resources.

Large Language Models

- **GPT-5 series (OpenAI, ~2-5T parameters):** Launched August 7, 2025, and positioned as a champion in versatility; handles everything from complex coding with multimodal capabilities (text/image/audio/video) to advanced reasoning and agentic workflows.

- **Claude Opus 4.5 (Anthropic, 130B+ parameters):** Known for thoughtful responses and massive context; excels at long documents.

- **PaLM 3 (Google, 340B parameters):** Strong multilingual and reasoning capabilities; well suited to long-context tasks (large inputs).

Small Language Models

- **Mistral 8x7B (now Mistral Large 2, 123B MoE):** Strong performance for its size; can run on 16GB GPUs.

- **Phi-4 (Microsoft, 14B parameters):** Trained on high-quality data and benchmarks; matches models up to 25x its size on reasoning tasks.

- **Llama 3.2 7B (Meta, 7B parameters):** Open-source foundation model for specialized industry variants.

Choosing the Right Model

Use LLMs when you need:

- Broad, general knowledge across domains
- Complex multi-step reasoning
- Creative and varied content generation
- Research and comprehensive analysis

Use SLMs when you need:

- Fast, local processing
- Privacy-sensitive applications

- Specific domain expertise
- Resource-efficient deployment
- Predictable, consistent outputs

The future isn't about choosing between large or small models – it's about using the right tool for each task. We're seeing SLMs becoming smarter through better training techniques, achieving performance that would have required massive models just a year ago. Simultaneously, modular AI systems are emerging where specialized models work together, each optimized for specific tasks.

This unlocks two parallel trends: personal AI assistants running entirely on your devices are becoming realistic because of SLMs, while LLMs continue to push the boundaries of what's possible in AI. The most successful implementations thoughtfully combine both approaches: LLMs for exploration and complex tasks, SLMs for deployment and specific applications.

In generative AI, the goal isn't to build the biggest model possible – it's to build the right model for each need. LLMs provide broad intelligence and creative capabilities that expand possibilities, while SLMs bring that intelligence to everyday devices efficiently and privately. Whether you're developing applications, optimizing business operations, or simply wanting AI assistance without cloud dependency, understanding when to use each type of model is crucial for success in the AI-powered future.

7.5.5 The Training Process

LLMs begin life knowing nothing - their parameters are randomly initialized. Through training, they gradually develop understanding.

- **Pre-training** involves exposing the model to vast amounts of text – books, websites, academic papers, code repositories, and more. The model learns to predict what comes next in a sequence, adjusting its parameters when wrong. This simple objective – predicting the next word – forces the model to learn grammar, facts, reasoning patterns, and even creative writing styles.

- **Fine-tuning** is the process of adapting a pre-trained model to perform specific tasks by training it further on high-quality, task-specific data. This can involve refining the model to follow instructions more accurately, maintain a helpful dialogue, or specialize in domains like medicine, law, or customer support.

- **Alignment** ensures the model behaves according to human values. Techniques like RLHF teach models to be helpful while avoiding harmful outputs, to admit uncertainty rather than fabricate information, and to respect ethical boundaries.

Capabilities and Limitations

Modern LLMs demonstrate remarkable capabilities:

- Natural language understanding across multiple languages
- Translation without explicit training for specific language pairs
- Code generation in dozens of programming languages
- Creative writing in various styles and formats
- Logical reasoning and problem-solving
- Question answering and information synthesis

But they also have fundamental limitations:

- No real-world experience or sensory input
- No persistent memory between conversations

- Can generate plausible-sounding but false information
- May reflect biases present in training data
- Limited context windows (though growing)
- No true understanding – only pattern matching at massive scale

Understanding these limitations helps you use LLMs effectively, knowing when to trust their output and when to verify.

7.6 Real-World Applications of GenAI

Let's move from theory to practice. How are businesses and individuals actually using generative AI to transform their work? I'll share concrete examples from various industries, showing not just what's possible but what's happening right now.

7.6.1 Healthcare

The healthcare industry has embraced generative AI in ways that are literally saving lives while reducing physician burnout.

Clinical documentation: Dr. Sarah Chen, a primary care physician in Seattle, shared her experience: "I used to spend 2–3 hours each evening completing patient notes. Now, an AI assistant listens to patient conversations (with consent) and generates structured clinical notes. I review and edit them, but what took hours now takes minutes. I actually get to have dinner with my family."

Diagnostic assistance: At Stanford Medical Center, radiologists use AI that analyzes medical images and generates detailed reports. The AI can spot patterns that might be missed during busy shifts, particularly effective at catching early-stage cancers and subtle abnormalities.

Figure 7.10 Trends in generative AI implementation in healthcare

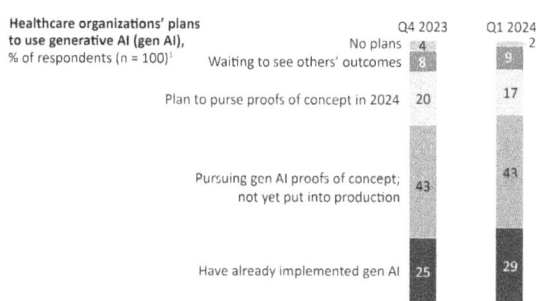

Healthcare organizations' plans to use generative AI (gen AI), % of respondents (n = 100)[1]

	Q4 2023	Q1 2024
No plans	4	2
Waiting to see others' outcomes	8	9
Plan to purse proofs of concept in 2024	20	17
Pursuing gen AI proofs of concept; not yet put into production	43	43
Have already implemented gen AI	25	29

Source: (Lamb et al., 2024).

McKinsey research reveals accelerating adoption of generative AI in healthcare, with implementation growing from 25% to 29% in just one quarter, and 43% of organizations actively pursuing proof-of-concept projects. This rapid adoption reflects the transformative impact seen in clinical settings.

Mental health support: AI chatbots trained in cognitive behavioral therapy techniques provide 24/7 support. While not replacing therapists, they offer immediate help during crisis moments and ongoing support between sessions.

7.6.2 Financial Services

The financial industry has found numerous applications for generative AI:

Automated analysis: Investment firms use AI to generate comprehensive market analyses in hours rather than weeks.

Personal financial planning: Banks deploy AI advisors that create personalized financial plans considering income, expenses, goals, and market conditions. These tools democratize access to financial planning previously available only to wealthy clients.

Fraud detection: AI systems generate synthetic fraud patterns to train better detection systems, identifying suspicious transactions in real-time and saving billions in losses.

Figure 7.11	AI-generated six-year financial forecast (2026–2032)

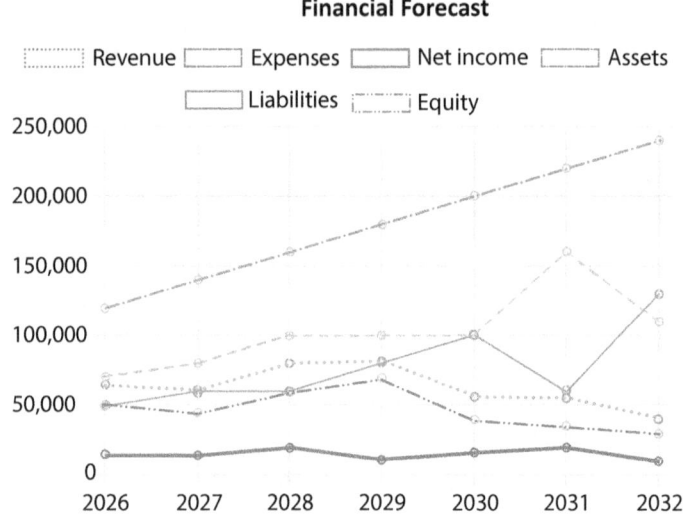

The above example of an AI-generated financial forecast shows revenue volatility, steady asset growth from $120K to $240K, emerging liability concerns, and fluctuating net income patterns. This demonstrates how generative AI democratizes sophisticated business analytics for companies of all sizes.

7.6.3 Education

Education is being transformed by AI that adapts to individual learning styles.

Intelligent tutoring: AI tutors provide personalized instruction 24/7, identifying where students struggle and adjusting their teaching approach accordingly.

Content creation: Teachers use AI to create lesson plans, quizzes, and differentiated materials for diverse classrooms in minutes rather than hours.

Language learning: Modern AI language tutors engage in conversations, correct pronunciation, explain grammar in context, and adapt to cultural nuances.

7.6.4 Creative Industries

Creative professionals are finding AI to be a powerful collaborator.

Writing: Professional writers use AI for brainstorming, overcoming writer's block, and exploring different narrative directions. It's like having a writing group available 24/7.

Music production: Musicians use AI to generate backing tracks, suggest chord progressions, and even master recordings, making professional production accessible to more creators.

Visual design: Designers use AI to generate initial concepts, create variations, and handle repetitive tasks, allowing more time for creative exploration.

7.6.5 Manufacturing and Industry

Manufacturing has found applications beyond the factory floor.

Generative design: Engineers input requirements, and AI generates thousands of design options, often creating organic shapes that minimize material while maximizing strength.

Predictive maintenance: AI analyzes sensor data to predict equipment failures before they happen, preventing costly downtime.

Supply chain optimization: AI simulates thousands of scenarios to optimize supply chains, considering cost, delivery time, risk, and environmental impact.

7.7 Conclusion

We've covered an enormous amount of ground in this chapter, right from understanding what generative AI is to exploring its history, mastering prompt engineering, examining real-world applications, and considering future possibilities. But this isn't the end of your AI journey – it's just the beginning.

The world of AI evolves rapidly. New models, applications, and discoveries emerge constantly. The key is to start experimenting, stay curious, and continue learning. Begin with small steps: try using AI for tasks you do regularly, experiment with different techniques, and share your discoveries.

Remember that AI is a tool, and like any tool, its value comes from how we use it. Use it to enhance your capabilities, not replace your thinking. Use it to create value for others, not just efficiency for yourself. Use it to solve real problems and make a positive impact. The future is being written right now, and with AI as your collaborator, you have the power to help write it.

 **Chapter Summary**

- Generative AI goes beyond recognizing patterns to creating entirely new content such as text, images, audio, video, and code. Its evolution spans from GANs (2014) to the Transformer breakthrough (2017), the rise of Large Language Models like GPT (2018–2020), the explosive public adoption of ChatGPT (2022–2023), and the current multimodal era (2024–2025) with specialized models and diverse applications.

- LLMs are massive AI models with billions to trillions of parameters, capable of general-purpose reasoning, creativity, and complex problem-solving. SLMs are smaller, faster, privacy-friendly models optimized for specific tasks and local deployment. Choosing between them depends on task complexity, resource availability, and privacy needs.

- Effective use of generative AI depends heavily on prompt engineering. Techniques include zero-shot, one-shot, few-shot, chain-of-thought, role-based, and iterative prompting. Crafting clear, specific, and structured prompts leads to better, more relevant outputs, while iterative refinement ensures high-quality results.

- Leading tools include OpenAI's ChatGPT (GPT-5.2, o-mini), Google's Gemini (3 Pro, 3 Flash), Anthropic's Claude (Opus 4.5), Meta's Llama 4 (open-source), and DeepSeek-V3.2. Each excels in different areas: versatility, real-time web access, structured reasoning, customization, or rapid multi-step problem-solving. Specialized tools like Midjourney, Stable Diffusion, Perplexity, and GitHub Copilot cater to creative, search, and coding needs.

- Generative AI is transforming healthcare (diagnostics, clinical documentation), financial services (fraud detection, forecasting), education (personalized tutoring, content creation), creative fields (writing, music, design), and manufacturing (generative design, predictive maintenance). It enhances productivity, enables creativity, and democratizes access to advanced analytics while requiring human oversight to address limitations like bias and hallucinations.

CHAPTER **8**

Ethical AI

Key Learning Objectives

- Understand the ethical dimensions of AI through the lens of real-world risks.
- Learn the importance of transparency and explainability in AI systems.
- Integrate ethical thinking across the AI lifecycle. Identify methods for detecting and mitigating bias.
- Learn how to design AI systems that uphold societal values, protect human rights, and prioritize inclusive development under ethical AI.

8.1 Introduction to Ethical AI

The ethics of AI falls under the ethics of advanced technology, concentrating on robots and other artificial intelligence agents. This can be categorized into roboethics (robot ethics) and machine ethics. Roboethics is focused on the ethical actions of individuals as they create, build, utilize, and engage/interact with the AI systems. In this chapter, we will understand the ethical concerns associated with AI, that may occur during the creation and implementation of

AI (e.g., human biases present in data, data privacy, and clarity), and moral concerns arising from AI (e.g., job loss and income disparity). Moreover, as machines grow increasingly intelligent and could potentially achieve consciousness in the future, we must take into account robot rights - the idea that individuals ought to have ethical responsibilities toward sentient machines.

As technology progresses and AI advances, robots or AI agents ought to exhibit moral behavior and demonstrate ethical principles. We view the moral conduct of AI agents as ethical AI. Currently, the most recognized regulations for guiding & governing AI agents are the Three Laws of Robotics presented by Isaac Asimov in the 1950s (Asimov, 1950).

The First Law states that a robot must not harm a human or, by its actions, inaction, permit a human to suffer. Second Law, a robot has to follow the commands issued to it by humans unless such commands conflict with the First Law. The Third Law, a robot must safeguard its survival as long as that safeguard does not contradict the First or Second Law.

8.1.1 The Real-World Consequences of Unethical AI

Recently, criminals leveraged AI-driven voice technology to mimic a CEO's voice and requested a deceptive transfer of $243,000 (Stupp, 2019). This isn't a singular event. PINDROP noted a 350% increase in voice fraud from 2013 to 2017 (Livni, 2019). AI voice imitation, the misuse of deepfake technology is not solely a matter of fraud. Deepfake involves a technique to overlay and combine existing images and videos with source images or videos using Machine Learning (ML), and is becoming increasingly prevalent. With Deepfake, human faces may be layered onto adult videos.

Content and political figures can be depicted in videos to provoke violence and fear. Scientists at the University of Washington developed a synthetic version of Obama by employing a neural network. AI was utilized to replicate the structure of Obama's mouth (BBC News, 2017). Although there was no security risk associated with the University of Washington experiment, the demonstration showcases what can be achieved with AI-modified videos. Misinformation is an additional worry. For instance, an AI text generator that produces false content was considered too risky to be launched by its developers, OpenAI, due to concerns over abuse. Clearly, sophisticated AI agents may place individuals, businesses, and communities in greater danger.

Human rights, including privacy, the right to associate, freedom of expression, the right to employment, non-discrimination and access to public services must always be prioritized. The increasing utilization of AI in the criminal justice system could raise concerns regarding discrimination. Risk-assessment software utilized throughout the criminal justice system reveals instances of bias based on ethnicity, gender, and race. For example, certain defendants are incorrectly categorized as high risk due to their race. The right to privacy, vital for human dignity, can also be influenced by AI.

8.1.2 What is Responsible AI?

Designing, creating, and implementing AI systems in a way that respects moral principles, fairness, safety, privacy, and accountability is called "responsible AI." According to Siau and Wang (2020), AI ethics can be divided into two categories: "ethical AI," which looks at how AI behaves ethically, and "ethics of AI," which focuses on how people create and use AI.

Every AI system is built on human decisions. Roboethics highlights that developers hold ethical responsibility ranging from protecting user privacy to making sure systems don't harm at-risk populations.

It's not merely about intelligent machines, but it's about ethical machines. Ethical AI examines how systems can be designed to act with honesty, even in intricate, real-world situations.

Machine ethics is about making AI capable of moral behavior. Is it possible for a machine to make an ethical decision? As we grant AI greater independence, we need to seriously consider how it can tell right from wrong and which ethical standards it should adhere to.

Aligning the behavior of AI agents with moral standards is essential. AI needs to be in harmony with human values. But which values? This challenge requires us to incorporate diverse perspectives when developing the regulations that govern AI.

Asimov's Three Laws must now be extended to include AI-to-AI ethical interaction. Today, we broaden them not only for human safety, but also to guide how AIs ought to interact with each other in a world they are increasingly sharing.

8.1.3 Core Ethical Principles for Responsible AI

- **Transparency:** Systems should be easy to understand. Because AI systems are often regarded as black boxes, the onus is on developers and other stakeholders to enhance transparency, from employing interpretable models to maintaining thorough documentation.
- **Fairness and non-discrimination:** AI systems must be regularly and proactively evaluated as well as adjusted

to prevent any societal biases related to race, gender, age or socioeconomic status.

- **Accountability:** When AI systems are responsible for any sort of damage or errors, they need to clearly take responsibility for AI based outcomes.

- **Safety and security:** AI must reduce potential harm; cyberattacks and misinformation show why strong protections are needed to prevent misuse.

- **Consent and privacy:** Individuals should have authority over their private information. AI systems need to ensure informed consent, manage data responsibly and hold privacy to the highest standard.

8.1.4 The Risks of Irresponsible AI

- **Discrimination due to data or algorithmic bias:** AI can unintentionally benefit certain groups over others, for example, approving loans for one race while rejecting another in case it is trained on such biased data. This can further reinforce or amplify existing social injustice due to discrimination.

- **Lack of transparency in decision-making processes:** When the decisions made by AI cannot be explained, then it becomes very hard to fix them. This lack of transparency can reduce trust and create significant harm, especially in domains like healthcare, hiring and justice.

- **Loss of independence, which results in manipulation:** Right from personalized ads to political content, AI can gently push what we consume, see or even think. With time, this reduces the critical thinking aspect which creates a world driven by algorithms over individual choice.

- **Absence of accountability:** Who bears the blame when AI malfunctions? When AI fails in sectors like healthcare or justice, without clear accountability, the victims are often left without clear answers.

- **Deepfakes as tools for spreading false information:** We have observed how AI-generated images, text, and videos can create believable misinformation. Deepfakes can damage reputation, manipulate the way voters think and create chaos within democracies.

- **AI-driven fraud using voice impersonation:** Scammers now use AI-generated voice imitation to impersonate victims' loved ones and deceive them into transferring money.

- **Fake news generation by powerful LLMs:** They can produce misleading articles at scale which makes it harder to identify the actual truth.

8.2 Bias in AI

Bias in AI is now a serious concern. One of the most well-known examples is COMPAS, a tool for risk assessment that was used in the US Criminal justice system, which was found to label Black defendants disproportionately as high-risk, even when they were not more likely to reoffend. Such instances show us how algorithms when trained on data with bias can increase societal inequalities. Therefore, ensuring fairness in AI systems needs a good understanding of ethics and social context in which the model is trained on.

AI systems may inherit human and societal biases, especially when it is trained on historical data where the prejudices exist. AI agents are only as good as the data humans train them with, and using datasets curated or created by humans, any existing biases maybe taken in, learned by AI agents and exhibited in real world applications. Using biased data for training can lead the AI system to make unfair or discriminatory choices in actual situations. For instance, predictive policing tools have demonstrated racial prejudice, frequently marking people from specific ethnic groups as high-risk (Bossmann, 2016). Thus, figuring out how to program and train AI agents without human biases is critical.

8.2.1 Types of Bias

Bias in AI can stem from multiple sources. While there are many forms, the following are among the most common types:

- **Data bias:** This mainly occurs when the training data reflects historical inequalities embedded in data. For example, the underrepresentation of women in tech leadership roles or minorities in healthcare data illustrates this bias. If this is not addressed, the AI learns and continues to repeat those patterns.

- **Algorithmic bias:** Even with a cleaner set of data, the model can develop bias during the training phase. How it weighs features for outcomes can unintentionally benefit certain groups over others if not properly addressed during the design phase.

- **Human bias:** Bias can also come from developers and users themselves. Whether during data labeling or algorithm design, these decisions often influence how the AI behaves.

8.2.2 Real-World Examples

- **Amazon recruitment tool:** Amazon created an AI recruitment tool that preferred resumes from males instead of females. The model learned from historical data, illustrating a male-centric tech industry, leading to systemic bias against female applicants.

- **Healthcare systems:** Skin cancer AI-diagnosis systems perform poorly on darker skin tones. Certain AI models designed for identifying skin cancer were mainly trained using images of patients with lighter skin tones over others. Consequently, these systems underperformed for individuals with darker skin, increasing their risk of misdiagnosis or treatment delays.

- **Finance:** Biased data is used by loan apps to reject minorities. Loan approval algorithms have utilized biased data that mirrors years of systemic discrimination. As a result, minority groups are unjustly denied credit, despite meeting the financial requirements

- **Marketing:** Advertisements algorithms have demonstrated a tendency to show women lower-paying job advertisements more often, whereas men encountered higher-paying positions. These prejudiced patterns perpetuate gender stereotypes and restrict economic prospects.

8.2.3 Techniques to Find and Reduce Bias

One of the first steps in addressing bias in AI is detecting it. The AIF360 library by IBM offers tools to measure fairness in datasets. Here's a simple example using gender and hiring decisions:

Step 1: Create a Sample Dataset

```
# Sample hiring data: 0 = Female, 1 = Male; 1 = Hired, 0 =
Not hired
import pandas as pd
df = pd.DataFrame({
    'gender': [0, 1, 0, 1, 1, 0],
    'hired': [0, 1, 0, 1, 1, 0]
})
```

Step 2: Load Data into AIF360's BinaryLabelDataset Format

BinaryLabelDataset is the core data structure used in AIF360 to evaluate fairness metrics.

```
from aif360.datasets import BinaryLabelDataset
dataset = BinaryLabelDataset(
    df=df,
    label_names=['hired'],
    protected_attribute_names=['gender']
)
```

Step 3: Define Privileged and Unprivileged Groups

In many real-world scenarios, we analyze how outcomes differ between such groups.

```
groups.privileged_groups = [{'gender': 1}]    # Typically
considered advantaged (e.g., Male)unprivileged_groups =
[{'gender': 0}]  # Typically disadvantaged (e.g., Female)
```

Step 4: Calculate Fairness Metric

Disparate Impact measures how the outcomes differ between groups. A value close to 1 indicates fairness. Values below 0.8 often suggest bias (as per the 80% rule in U.S. legal frameworks).

```
from aif360.metrics import BinaryLabelDatasetMetric
metric = BinaryLabelDatasetMetric(dataset,
privileged_groups=privileged_groups,
unprivileged_groups=unprivileged_groups)
print("Disparate Impact:", metric.disparate_impact())
```

If the Disparate Impact is significantly below 1, it may indicate that one group (e.g., women) is being treated unfairly in comparison to the other (e.g., men).

This technique is just the beginning, once bias is detected, AIF360 also supports pre-processing (data repair), in-processing (fair model training), and post-processing (adjusting outputs) to reduce bias.

8.3 Transparency and Explainability

Understanding an AI model's decision is just as crucial as the correctness of that decision. In critical domains such as healthcare, finance, and recruitment, a lack of clear explanations for outcomes can result in distrust, legal problems, or actual harm. When sophisticated models such as deep neural networks generate outputs, they frequently function as black boxes—precise, yet unclear. In comparison, white-box models such as decision trees provide clarity but might not possess the capabilities of more intricate structures.

Table 8.1 Black-box vs. white-box models

Model Type	Examples	Characteristics
Black-box	Deep Neural Networks, Ensemble Models	High accuracy, low interpretability
White-box	Decision Trees, Rule-Based Systems	Transparent logic, easy to explain

Black-box models are harder to interpret directly, which is where explainable AI (XAI) tools come in.

8.3.1 Popular Tools for Model Explainability

- **SHAP (SHapley Additive exPlanations):** SHAP helps explain how much each feature (like age, income, etc.) contributed to a model's prediction. It's based on a fair system from game theory. It considers every feature as a "participant" or a player in a team game, and

SHAP calculates how much each player helped the team in winning (i.e. make a prediction). This approach guarantees equality and uniformity, and it is especially useful for complex models such as XGBoost or neural networks, that are otherwise hard to interpret.

- **LIME (Local Interpretable Model-agnostic Explanations):** This method explains predictions by slightly modifying the input data and observing how the model's output changes. It then applies a basic model (such as linear regression) just around that example to explain what the main model was doing. This helps in clarifying individual predictions, even if the overall model is too intricate to comprehend entirely.

LIME and SHAP serve the common goal of making AI decisions interpretable, but their underlying methodologies present fundamental distinctions that influence how and what they explain. Let's look at the comparative view below.

Table 8.2 Comparison of LIME and SHAP for model explainability

Feature	LIME	SHAP	Key Difference
Approach	Local approximation using simpler models	Game theory concepts for feature attribution	LIME focuses on local behavior, while SHAP focuses on overall impact
Explanation Type	Local explanations	Both local and global explanations	SHAP provides broader interpretability
Computation Speed	Generally faster	Can be more computationally intensive	LIME is quicker for individual predictions
Consistency	Can be less stable	Mathematically consistent	SHAP offers more reliable results across multiple runs

Source: (Wilson, 2024).

Why Explainability Matters

- It builds **trust** in AI systems among users and stakeholders.

- It supports **regulatory compliance** (e.g., GDPR's "right to explanation").

- It helps **debug models** and uncover hidden biases.

- It improves **collaboration** between data scientists and domain experts.

8.3.2 Explaining Predictions with SHAP with Sample Code

Let's walk through a basic example using SHAP with an XGBoost classifier trained on a breast cancer dataset:

```
# Importing libraries
import shap, xgboost
from sklearn.model_selection import train_test_split
from sklearn.datasets import load_breast_cancer
```

Sample snapshot of data

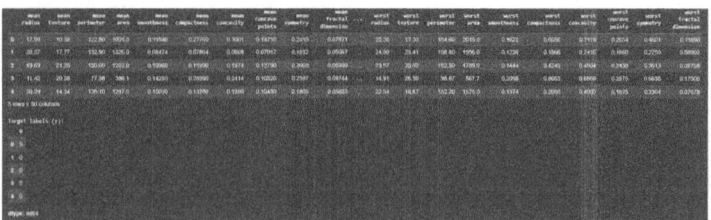

```
# Load and split the dataset
X, y = load_breast_cancer(return_X_y=True)
X_train, X_test, y_train, y_test = train_test_split(X, y,
test_size=0.2)
# Train a black-box model
model = xgboost.XGBClassifier().fit(X_train, y_train)
# Initialize SHAP explainer
```

```
explainer = shap.Explainer(model)
# Compute SHAP values for the test data
shap_values = explainer(X_test)
# Visualize the contribution of features for a single
  prediction
shap.plots.waterfall(shap_values[0])
```

The waterfall plot reveals how individual features either increase or decrease the model's confidence in a prediction, making even black-box decisions more transparent.

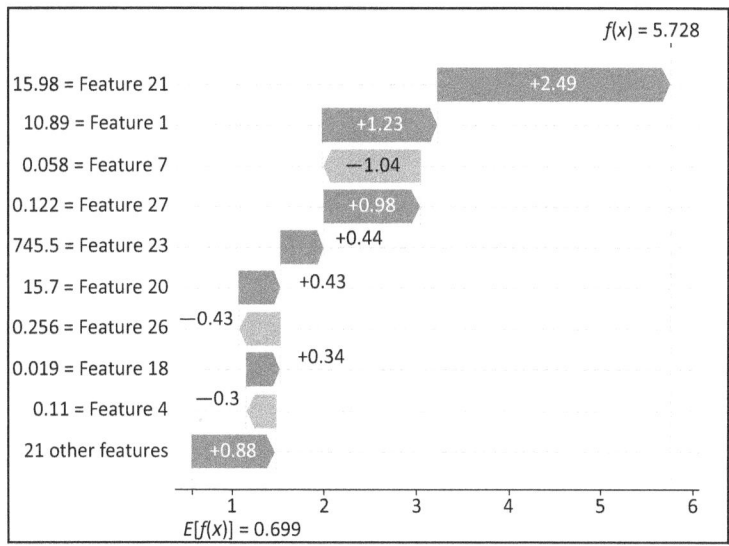

8.4 Governance in AI

With AI being a part of decision-making across various sectors, robust governance is crucial to guarantee that these systems adhere to ethical, legal, and societal standards. Organizations are now actively establishing governance frameworks. These might involve ethics committees, accountable AI groups, and established guidelines as per global best practices and standards. To instill accountability and trust, we need:

- **Routine assessments:** Scheduled reviews of AI systems to detect bias, performance shifts, or unforeseen outcomes.

- **Model cards:** Written materials that outline a model's purpose, effectiveness, constraints, and ethical implications in a detailed structure.

- **Datasheets for datasets:** A clear account of the methods used for data collection, processing, and labeling - encouraging ethical data utilization.

- **Transparency guidelines:** Explicit records of decision-making processes, feature significance, and system operations to promote stakeholder confidence.

8.4.1 Global Frameworks and Guidelines

From healthcare privacy to inclusive design, these frameworks reflect each region's priorities and challenges. Collectively, they create a global ethical baseline that helps remind us that while AI may be technical, its impact is deeply human.

- **EU AI Act:** Risk classification & accountability. It categorizes AI systems by risk level and mandates responsibility and oversight, particularly for high-risk sectors such as healthcare and law enforcement.

- **IEEE Guidelines:** Human well-being, education, and effectiveness. They emphasize the need for AI to enhance human welfare, support education and individual development, and deliver measurable, reliable outcomes.

- **AI4People:** Beneficence, justice, explicability. This framework introduces fundamental ethical principles such as beneficence (promoting good), non-maleficence (preventing harm), justice, explicability, and autonomy.

- **UNESCO AI ethics recommendation:** It supports human dignity, inclusiveness, and the "do no harm" principle, while promoting cultural and global equity.

Multiple global organizations have established ethical guidelines and regulatory structures to steer the development and application of AI:

- **HIPAA (Health Insurance Portability and Accountability Act):** While not AI-specific, HIPAA imposes strict rules on data privacy and security in healthcare. Any AI system processing medical data in the U.S. must be compliant with HIPAA, making it a key legal touchpoint.

- **DPDP Act (Digital Personal Data Protection Act, 2023):** India's landmark data protection law enforces user consent, purpose limitation, and data minimization—key principles for ethical AI that handles personal data.

8.5 Designing Ethical AI Systems

Ethics in AI cannot be an afterthought but it must be built into the AI system from the very beginning. Responsible AI requires intentional and conscious design across every stage of the machine learning lifecycle in problem solving. Especially in high-risk domains such as healthcare, finance, and criminal justice, these systems demand even higher standards. In such cases, integrating a "human in the loop" concept ensures that critical decisions are verified or overridden by SMEs/ humans, not just left to automated outputs.

8.5.1 Lifecycle Integration

Each stage in the AI lifecycle presents opportunities to embed ethical safeguards.

- **Data collection:** Ensure diverse and representative datasets. Avoid over-representing or removing certain groups by applying any sort of bias checks.
- **Model training:** Use bias testing and detection algorithms to evaluate fairness. Tools like AIF360 or SHAP can help identify and reduce skewness in model outcomes.
- **Deployment:** Implement logging and obtain user consent so that users know when they are interacting with AI and how their data is being used.
- **Monitoring:** Set up periodic checks and audits to ensure the model is safe in real-world conditions.

8.5.2 Example: Ethical Logging for Transparency

A simple logging mechanism can ensure traceability of predictions, which is critical in regulated or high-stakes environments. If a user disputes a decision, logs provide an auditable trail at any point in time, which is key to transparency and accountability.

```
# Import libraries
import logging
from datetime import datetime
logging.basicConfig(filename='audit_log.txt', level=logging.
INFO)
# Sample input and prediction
input_data = {'age': 45, 'income': 55000}
prediction = 'High Risk'
# Log the decision with timestamp
logging.info(f"{datetime.now()} - Input: {input_data},
Prediction: {prediction}")
```

8.5.3 Consent Mechanism UI Snippet

It's essential to inform users when they're engaging with an AI system (be it chatbot or any automated assistant) and get their explicit consent. Consent isn't just a legal checkbox but it's a signal of respect for user autonomy and awareness.

Consent goes beyond being a legal necessity, it's an indication of respect for the user's independence, openness, and digital integrity.

An effectively crafted consent system guarantees:

- **Transparency:** Users must immediately recognize that they are engaging with AI.
- **Option:** Users should have the ability to make a meaningful choice to participate or refrain.
- **Trust:** Openness promotes a more secure and ethical AI interaction.

Example mockup:

You are interacting with an AI system. Do you consent to this interaction?

 Yes ✘ No

8.6 Conclusion

Comprehending and tackling ethical and moral concerns associated with AI remains in the early stages. AI ethics is not merely concerned with "right or wrong," "good or bad," and "virtue or vice." It does not even represent a challenge that can be addressed by a limited number of individuals. However, ethical and moral concerns pertaining to AI are essential and require immediate discussion. This chapter highlights the pressing need for diverse stakeholders to focus on the ethics and morality of AI agents. As we work to shape principles that enable the development of ethical AI, we must also deepen our understanding of human ethics, refine current ethical standards, and improve our engagement with AI systems in this AI age.

AI ethics must be a primary focus in the creation of AI agents, rather than a secondary concern. The future of humankind could rely on the proper establishment of AI ethics!

Chapter Summary

- Ethical AI encompasses both roboethics (responsibilities of AI creators and users) and machine ethics (ensuring AI agents act morally). Core principles include transparency, fairness, accountability, safety, and privacy, supported by frameworks like Asimov's Three Laws and modern global AI governance guidelines.

- Irresponsible AI can lead to discrimination, bias, lack of transparency, manipulation, loss of accountability, deepfakes, fraud, and large-scale misinformation. Real-world incidents demonstrate how AI misuse can harm individuals, businesses, and democratic systems.

- AI bias can arise from data, algorithms, or human decisions. Examples include gender bias in recruitment tools, racial disparities in justice systems, and medical misdiagnosis due to unrepresentative datasets. Tools like IBM's AIF360 can detect and mitigate bias through pre-, in-, and post-processing techniques.

- Building trust in AI requires clear explanations for decisions, especially in critical domains. Methods like SHAP and LIME help interpret complex "black-box" models by revealing feature contributions and local decision logic, supporting fairness, compliance, and debugging.

- Ethical safeguards must be embedded across the AI lifecycle: diverse data collection, bias-aware training, consent-based deployment, and continuous monitoring. Governance practices (e.g., model cards, datasheets, audits) and global ethical frameworks ensure AI aligns with societal values, protects human rights, and fosters inclusive development.

References

Altman, S. (2023, May 22). *Testimony before the U.S. Senate Committee on the Judiciary. OpenAI.* https://openai.com/blog/sam-altman-testimony

Asimov, I. (1950). Runaround. In *I, Robot* (The Isaac Asimov Collection ed.). Doubleday.

BBC News. (2017). *Fake Obama created using AI video tool* [YouTube video]. YouTube. https://www.youtube.com/watch?v=AmUC4m6w1wo

Bossmann, J. (2016). *Top 9 ethical issues in artificial intelligence. World Economic Forum.* https://www.weforum.org/ethical-issues-in-AI

Coleman, T. (2018). *Photograph shot in Kenya* [Photograph]. Instagram.

Crevier, D. (1993). *AI: The tumultuous history of the search for artificial intelligence.* Basic Books.

Domingos, P. (2015). *The master algorithm: How the quest for the ultimate learning machine will remake our world.* Basic Books.

Gates, B. (2019, March 21). *AI can help society overcome the challenges of inequality. Gates Notes.* https://www.gatesnotes.com/AI

Google. (n.d.). *About Google.* https://about.google/

Hendler, J. (2008). Avoiding another AI winter. *IEEE Intelligent Systems*, 23(2), 2–4. https://doi.org/10.1109/MIS.2008.28

IBM Research. (n.d.). *AI Explainability 360.* https://aix360.mybluemix.net/

Lamb, J., Israelstam, G., Agarwal, R., & Bhasker, S. (2024, July 25). *Generative AI in healthcare: Adoption trends and what's next. McKinsey & Company.* https://www.mckinsey.com/industries/healthcare/our-insights/generative-ai-in-healthcare-adoption-trends-and-whats-next

LIME. (n.d.). *Local interpretable model-agnostic explanations.* https://github.com/marcotcr/lime

Livni, E. (2019). *A new kind of cybercrime uses AI and your voice against you. Quartz.* https://qz.com/1699819/a-new-kind-of-cybercrime-uses-ai-and-your-voice-against-you/

McCarthy, J., Minsky, M., Rochester, N., & Shannon, C. (1955). *A proposal for the Dartmouth summer research project on artificial intelligence.* Dartmouth College.

McCarthy, J. (1956). *Proposal for the Dartmouth Summer Research Project on Artificial Intelligence.* Dartmouth College.

Nilsson, N. J. (2010). *The quest for artificial intelligence: A history of ideas and achievements.* Cambridge University Press.

OpenAI. (n.d.). *About OpenAI.* https://openai.com/

OpenCog Foundation. (n.d.). *OpenCog project.* https://opencog.org/

PayPal. (n.d.). *About PayPal*. https://about.pypl.com/

Ribeiro, M. T., Singh, S., & Guestrin, C. (2016). "Why should I trust you?" Explaining the predictions of any classifier. In *Proceedings of the 22nd ACM SIGKDD International Conference on Knowledge Discovery and Data Mining (KDD '16)* (pp. 1135–1144). https://doi.org/10.1145/2939672.2939778

SHAP. (n.d.). *SHapley Additive exPlanations*. https://shap.readthedocs.io/

Siau, K., & Wang, W. (2020). Artificial intelligence (AI) ethics. *Journal of Database Management*, 31, 74–87. https://doi.org/10.4018/JDM.2020040105

Stupp, C. (2019). *Fraudsters used AI to mimic CEO's voice in unusual cybercrime case. The Wall Street Journal*. https://www.wsj.com/articles/fraudsters-use-ai-to-mimic-ceos-voice-in-unusualcybercrime-case-11567157402

Takyar, A. (2023). *What is deep learning, and how does it work? LeewayHertz*. https://www.leewayhertz.com/what-is-deep-learning/

Turing, A. M. (1950). Computing machinery and intelligence. *Mind*, 59(236), 433–460. https://doi.org/10.1093/mind/LIX.236.433

Vertex AI. (n.d.). *Google Cloud Vertex AI*. https://cloud.google.com/vertex-ai

Wilson. (2024). *Understanding AI decisions: LIME vs SHAP. Medium*. https://smilewilson1999-73128.medium.com/understanding-ai-decisions-lime-vs-shap-52919b8d55dc

Glossary

Accountability: Holding developers and users responsible for AI impacts.

Activation Function: A function that determines if a neuron should be activated.

Algorithm: A set of rules or instructions given to an AI to help it learn from data.

Artificial General Intelligence (AGI): AI with human-level understanding and intellectual capabilities across various domains.

Artificial Neural Network (ANN): Computation model inspired by the human brain's interconnected neuron structure.

Automation: Using technology to perform tasks without human intervention.

Backpropagation: The process of training a neural network by adjusting weights backward from the output.

Bias: Systematic errors in AI that lead to unfair outcomes.

Classification: Assigning inputs into categories.

Clustering: Grouping similar data points together.

Computer Vision (CV): AI enabling machines to interpret and understand visual information.

Convolution: A mathematical operation used in CNNs to detect features.

Convolutional Neural Network (CNN): Neural networks specialized for processing grid-like data such as images.

Dataset: A collection of data points.

Decision Tree: A model using branching methods to illustrate decisions.

Deep Learning: A subset of machine learning using layered neural networks.

Diffusion Models: AI models used to generate images by gradually denoting data.

Epoch: One complete pass through the training dataset.

Ethical AI: Principles guiding responsible AI development and use.

Explainability: Ability to explain how and why an AI made a decision.

Feature: An individual measurable property or characteristic of the phenomenon being observed.

Feature Extraction: Identifying important aspects or patterns in an image.

Fairness: Ensuring AI treats all groups fairly.

Generative AI: AI models that create new content like text, images, and music.

Gradient Descent: An optimization algorithm for finding the minimum value of a function, often used in training AI models.

Hyperparameter: Settings that influence how an AI model learns.

Image Classification: Identifying objects within an image.

Image Segmentation: Dividing an image into parts to simplify analysis.

Imbalanced Data: When one class of data significantly outnumbers the other in a dataset.

Interpretability: Understanding and explaining the decisions made by AI models.

Input Layer: The first layer in a neural network, where data enters the model.

Label: The output or target variable in supervised learning.

Language Model: A model that predicts the likelihood of sequences of words.

Large Language Model (LLM): Pre-trained models like GPT that generate human-like text.

Machine Learning (ML): A subset of AI enabling machines to learn from data.

Model: A mathematical representation of a system, learned by AI from data.

Model Overfitting: When a model performs well on training data but poorly on new data.

Named Entity Recognition (NER): Detecting and classifying proper names in text.

Natural Language Processing (NLP): The branch of AI dealing with understanding and generating human language.

Neural Network: A series of algorithms modeled on the human brain, designed to recognize patterns.

Object Detection: Locating and classifying objects within images or videos.

Overfitting: When a model performs well on training data but poorly on new data.

Optimization: The process of improving a model's performance by tuning its parameters.

Part-of-Speech Tagging: Identifying the grammatical parts of words.

Privacy: Protecting individuals' data used by AI systems.

Prompt Engineering: Crafting inputs to guide generative AI outputs.

Regression: Predicting continuous values.

Reinforcement Learning: Learning through trial-and-error using feedback from actions.

Regulation: Legal frameworks governing AI use.

Sentiment Analysis: Determining the emotional tone behind a body of text.

Support Vector Machine (SVM): A classifier that finds the best boundary between classes.

Testing Data: Data used to evaluate the AI after training.

Tokenization: Breaking text into smaller units like words or sentences.

Transparency: Openness about how AI systems make decisions.

Training Data: The data used to teach AI algorithms.

Underfitting: When a model is too simple to capture the patterns in data.

Vector: A mathematical object representing data in a multidimensional space.

Visual Recognition: The process of identifying and categorizing visual data such as images or videos.

Weights: Parameters in a neural network that influence the strength of connections between neurons.